WILCOX

NORDIC JOURNEYS

The Revised Fifth Edition
of Viking Journey to Happiness

by TERRY PLANT

ISBN 0 9510511 2 1

Reprinted 1993

Also by Terry Plant

TRAIN JOURNEYS IN VIKING LANDS
(ISBN 0 9510511 0 5)

For Children

THE HAPPY LITTLE TRAIN

HENRY THE GOAT

LEIF THE REINDEER

Published by:
Terry Plant, 11, Lyndhurst Avenue, Kingskerswell, Newton Abbot,
Devon TQ12 5AJ, England

Printed by:
Short Run Press Ltd., Exeter, Devon, England

ACKNOWLEDGEMENTS.

No man has really lived until he has looked into the heart of Nature and has learned to appreciate the magnificent World on which he has been created.

Life is many ways like a journey, and often, by our own sincere efforts and the kindness of other fellow-travellers, we can make our lives a true journey to happiness.

It is also true that joy in living, friendships, love and sentiment enrich ennoble our daily life. Just as the French sing of their love and emotions so many of us express the same love and sentiment when we see a magnificent sunset over the fjords or the delicate and varied hues of Autumn in the forests and mountains. Nature has blessed these Viking lands in a thousand ways, from the gentle dew of a Summer morning or the sparkling frost of a Winter day. Here one finds such stillness that one can almost hear Nature speak, a certain stillness which gives one peace of mind and inner joy and renewed strength for the everyday life.

Sincere gratitude is given to the Norwegian, Swedish, Finnish, Danish, and Icelandic embassies in London, and the useful information of the Norwegian, Finnish, Swedish, and Danish State Railways.

But, above all, one is inspired with the Spirit of the People of these Nordic lands.

Cloudberries (Molter) R.P.

COLOUR PLATES

BLACK AND WHITE PHOTOGRAPHS

(Colour Photography, except Page 112, by Rosemary Plant)

CONTENTS

PREFACE

Having lived and worked, and travelled extensively, in the Nordic lands I share with you my love for and knowledge of Scandinavia. In the following pages I have written of Nordic cities and towns, and described beautiful journeys through some of Scandinavia's finest scenery and most interesting districts.

Terry Plant

NORWAY THE SUBLIME

CHAPTER 1

NORWAY THE SUBLIME

As early Spring returned I sailed from the busy port of Newcastle on the Bergen Line ship "Leda". It was a truly eventful journey, experiencing the changing of the seasons in Scandinavia, the snow-bound landscapes of the mountains in early Spring, the splendid, hot days of the height of Summer, and the gradual change of the Autumn splendour of the northern forests. Stavanger, on the west coast of the fjiord country, was my first port of call, and although the ship only stayed here three hours I was able to walk by the harbourside, and through the narrow, tidy streets, with their surrounding clusters of neatly painted cottages nestling amongst the rocky, steep hillsides.

These fishermen's cottages, soundly built of timber and painted in a fascinating variety of colours possess a true dignity of their own. Many a brave seaman has risked his life wrestling with the sea, and many of these warm and hospitable homes can tell many tales of hope, sadness, and wondrous joy, discomforts and hardships, and safe returns to this peaceful haven surrounded by a multitude of fjiords and rugged coast with its windswept islands.

In a small cafe by the harbour I enjoyed some very hot coffee, and wrote some hurried lines to my Mother. I enjoyed looking at the local fishermen who were enjoying a friendly drawn-out conversation. The Leda was once more on the high seas winding amongst the islands with their small villages and sometimes quite extensive forests. To the right rose high, steep mountains, their snow-capped peaks shining brightly in the sunshine it was a truly magnificent vista.!! By late afternoon we approached Bergen, and the surrounding mountains were partly enveloped in low clouds and thick mist, so typical of the west coast. How different it is in May, when bright sunshine and clear blue skies turn it into a rhapsody of bright colours.!!

As I walked along the busy streets of Bergen, a gradual thaw had set in, the water dripped incessently from the high roof tops and the streets were full of heaped up piles of melting snow. The people hurrying home from work, looked rather tired, and judging by their facial expressions and warm clothing, I could tell that they too longed for the speedy return of Springtime. I found my way to a cafe overlooking the harbour. As I looked at the coastal steamers, fishing smacks, and homeward-bound workers, I relaxed completely, and a feeling of peace and contentment filled me with unexpected radiant joy.!! Then it was time to board the train to Oslo, a three hundred mile journey over some of Norway's most spectacular scenery.

The Bergen railway which connects the west coast with Norway's capital, is a wonder in every aspect, the unending variety of scenery, and the tremendous skill and determination of Norwegian engineers in constructing it.!! During the long Winters, this line is the sole means of communication by land between east and west Norway. This journey traverses landscapes, ranging from smiling meadows and rich farmlands to mountains well above the limit of tree growth. After emerging from the long Ulriken tunnel, the train followed the calm waters of the Sorfjord for many miles, before heading east towards the mountains. The Ulriken tunnel is five miles long, and is the longest of the two hundred on this line. Voss was an important stopping point, this popular tourist centre is on the northern shores of Lake Vangsvatn, and is amidst the vast forests and higher slopes of the mountains.

It was just like a Christmas greeting, looking out from my warm compartment unto the snowy landscape, frozen lakes, and deep pine forests, under a bright full moon. Slowly the train climbed up towards the high Hardanger plateau, the forests became scantier, until only snow and dark rocky crags predominated. At the station of Myrdal the snow was piled high, it serves the Flam line, which in a mere twelve miles descends nearly three thousand feet to the Flam station on the Aurland fjord. It is rather unique for a normal standard line railway, as the steepest gradient is one in eighteen.

The Flam line passes through 20 tunnels with a total length of 3.7 miles, and at the finest views the train slows down or makes a brief halt to enable passengers to enjoy their journey as much as possible. For the first mile or two the Flam line runs through a series of snowsheds almost parallel to the Oslo-Bergen line, and at Vatnahalsen the view over the steeply sloping Flam valley with the high surrounding mountains, capped by perpetual snow, has to be seen to be believed. And between Kjosfossen and Bakli tunnel the train crosses a long embankment where swift waters cascade from ledge to ledge below with untamed majesty. The last thousand feet descent from the Myrdal mountain to the level of the Aurlands fjord is negotiated by a reverse tunnel, so that in all the line runs at five levels within a point to point distance of 0.6. mile. Before entering the longest tunnel, Nali, I, 476 yards long, the most spectacular scenery is passed. While the train stands at the fourth level, the other three levels of the line can be seen, and also the steep road which climbs Myrdals berg in 21 turns.!! Finally, at Hareina the valley widen out, here are well-kept farmsteads and the Flam church. Flam station is at the head of the Aurlands fjord, which joins the Sognefjord, 112 miles in length, and Norways greatest. The luxuriant growth in Summer, especially the orchards of apples, plums and cherries, and beech and oak trees, show the mildness of the coastal area.

The highest stretch was reached at Finse, with an altitude well over 4,000 feet, the desolate fells, devoid of any sign of human habitation, gave one a strange feeling of awe and majesty. Further eastwards, at just over 3,000 feet, the first thickets of dwarf mountain birch appeared, it is a marvel how they can grow in the very brief Summer and survive the in-

The author at Vatnahalsen on the scenic Flam Railway.

BERGEN—Always bids you welcome.

tense cold. Everywhere were frozen lakes, even the surfaces of the mountain streams were completely frozen over. As the train entered the fertile, thickly forested Hallingdal valley, a few lights shone brightly from remote hillside farms. By the time the train made a lengthy halt at Honefoss, it was full daylight. The whole landscape was still in the depths of Winter and on arrival at Oslo a driving snowstorm had swiftly descended on the town. Anne, a plump jovial nurse from the Ulleval hospital met me at the station and drove me to the recently built Haraldsheim Youth Hostel. I took an instant liking to this modern, spacious building on the north-eastern approaches to the city. The view over the spreading town, the Oslo fjord, the nearby Holmenkollen mountain came as a wonderful surprise.

Countless times I have gained inspiration from this splendid view, especially at sunset, when the northern sky is a glow with splendid, slowly changing colours, and the distant lights of the town's gradually join in this calm, unspoilt change from twilight into night.!! I love the vista best in the early Spring and Autumn, especially the latter, when the mellow colours and clear atmosphere are a joy beyond compare. This is a masterpiece of painting, where Nature, and not man, is the Divine painter.

My first contact was with Erwen, the friendly, hard-working caretaker. Several times I have been to his home, to meet his charming English wife Molly, and his two delightful children, Per and Kari. At the weekend Anne showed me something of Oslo and its splendid surroundings, the nights were still bitterly cold. And so it was time to continue my journey to Gothenburg. and commence work as a gardener. How good it was to be once more at Stora Katrinelund Youth Hostel and meet some of of my old friends. But my luck was out, for the ground was still frozen, so I hiked north to Oslo in search fo work.

I soon found work at the dockyards, my first task was unloading a large consignment of fruit, which I quite enjoyed. But unloading scrap-iron was beyond a joke, the dust and dirt seemed to penetrate every shred of my working clothing.!! Also the work was too erratic, sometimes there were few ships in dock, and I would wander the streets of Oslo, feeling rather sorry for myself. However, I was fortunate enough to obtain a small sum for an article on my travels which I wrote for the newspaper "Aftenposten". And after enquiring about work at the hotel "Viking" I commenced work as a dishwasher. This work I found rather monotonous and irksome, especially the late shift, which meant work until midnight from early afternoon. Still, even this had its compensations, as I could visit the National Art Gallery, the Deichmans Library with its numerous English Books and magazines, or take a trip with Anne to the surrounding mountains. I enjoyed her company and wonderful, sense of humour.

During this five-week stay in Oslo I got to know more about the Norwegians, their way of life and fine democracy. And with this knowledge came a greater understanding and fondness. The Norwegians are individualistic and liberal-socialists, and their ideals, and respect for mankind have almost completely eliminated strikes and unemployment. Goodwill and tolerance pervades amongst all ranks of industry, factories, farms, and forest are substantial sources of income, as do the exports of machinery, foods and furniture.

Norway depends on the sea for her progress and prosperity She has the fourth largest merchant navy in the World, which is no small achievement for a nation with under four million inhabitants. Norway builds many of her ships herself, but Sweden, Germany, and Britain also supply her with valuable cargo ships. In every port you will find a ship waving the Norwegian flag, and this brings progress and well-being to a multitude of other lands. Thanks to the warming influence of the Gulf Stream throughout the Winter her ports are virtually ice-free, even well beyond the Arctic Circle. Other areas, such as much of Canada and Siberia have not this warm current of water flowing northward, and are under perma-frost, which reaches even as far south as the latitude of Paris in Siberia. I prefer the south-east of Norway, where the climate is drier than the west coast, with colder Winters and warmer Summers. Towns like Bodo and Tromso, well above the Arctic Circle, are no colder than Lillehammar and Oslo, but much cooler in Summer. Huge forests cover the south and east of Norway, more forests have been planted over a long period, so this does much to encourage employment and a stable economy. Hydro-electric power is a superabundant source of energy, and some of this power, harnessed from the many swiftly flowing rivers, is even exported to Sweden.

A rapid change took place towards the end of April. The sun gained strength during the longer days, and the snow thawed with a speed which was truly amazing. The trees in the city's parks showed their first tender green buds, while crocuses, snowdrops and rock-plants burst forth into flower. Now and again I would be given a free day from work, and often spent an hour or two, just basking in the warm sunshine, a boon to any Soul living in the North.!! And as May came, I made up my mind to return to Gothenburg, that bustling port which is still my most beloved town in the whole of Sweden.

Throughout the Summer I worked as a free-lance gardener often cycling several miles to work. Cycling on the outskirts of the town was very fascinating, especially early in the morning, watching the red squirrels leap amongst the lofty tree branches, hear the song of the birds, and smell the freshness of the dew or freshness of the rain. Gothenburg can be very wet at times, but the rain is also refreshing and cooling, and the wet spells are soon followed by brilliantly sunny and warm days. I would often cycle to work and pass through the busy harbourside, and have a quick cup of coffee at a dockyard cafe.

Stora Katrinelund Youth Hostel was close to the shopping centre, the docklands and the railway station, so was very well situated. And each evening I would make tea or coffee and have some delightful meetings with people of many nations. The hostel warden, Sigurd Lie, was a Norwegian with an abundant humour, vitality, and good-will. The receptionist, Aino Hanski, was a Russian, who survived the terrible blockade of Leningrad, and was later captured and used as forced labour by the Germans. He was a humanitarian and an idealist and believed that in every nation exists forces for goodness and progress. He has had a book published about his experiences, as he believes writing can be a sincere way way of expressing one's views and influence others for good.!!

After finishing my season's work in Gothenburg, I left in early September and hitch-hiked to Norway. After several rather short lifts, luck came my way.!! Not far from the Norwegian frontier a small car with three young nurses from South Africa stopped, and even though part of the back seat was packed with luggage, they were pleased to offer me a place. I was able to help them by giving them useful information and helping them to find a place at Haraldsheim youth hostel. During the evening I acted as a guide for them, showing them something of Oslo, and its splendid surroundings. They were overjoyed with the view from the Holmenkollen mountain, and a light refreshment at an open-air cafe in the park of Studenterlunden, in the busy town-centre. I would have liked to have spent a few days in Oslo, but they had decided to continue with their journey towards Bergen, the following day.

The forest trees had already took on their first Autumn colours and we passed by numerous villas with their large gardens quite close to the Oslo fjord. The sea was calm, under a clear blue sky, everywhere the colours were varied and intense. As we headed west, through the thickly forested Hallingdal valley, we caught our first glimpse of new snow on a distant mountain peak. We spent the night at Geilo a popular winter resort. I took a long walk in the evening, the mountain air was cold but invigorating. Next day the scenery was spectacular, and as we slowly ascended towards the high mountains of the Hardanger plateau, the dwarf birch forests gradually became sparse, to be replaced by vast tracts of lonely moors, mountain passes, and swiftly flowing streams, and numerous small lakes. Here only a few clumps of grass, mosses and lichens survived, and as we passed the mighty Voringsfoss falls the sound was almost deafening.

A steep descent with a seeminly unending series of hairpin bends on the sides of almost vertical cliffs made it the most nerve-racking trip that I had ever made in Norway, and I quietly breathed a sigh of relief as we reached lower ground. At Eidfjord we were once again at sea level, and stopped for a pick-nick, making coffee with the aid of a primus stove. The towering mountains looked rather cold and dreary, as the sky was overcast and misty, high waterfalls flung their rushing torrents over the steeply inclining slopes, I felt chilly in the damp atmosphere. How I cheered to the warmth of the lounge on the ferry which brought us to Kinsarvik.

Soon the clouds dispersed, and the sun transformed the scene into one of superb splendour. For we were now in the region of the Hardanger Fjord, with its deep blue waters, green pastures, wooded hills, mirrowed against a background of mountains, gleaming white with eternal snow. Orchards, their trees laden with ripe fruit, grew close to the water's edge, and farmers with their families, old and young, were busy with the harvest. Horses are still very numerous, as the sloping land is often unsuitable for the use of tractors. Many important artists have painted scenes from the Hardanger fjord, and each Spring and Summer thousands of visitors from all corners of the World spend their holidays here.

After passing beautiful villages such as Oystese and Norheimsund we reached Bergen. And the town of Bergen had been the beginning and termination of a unique and highly enjoyable holiday. And during this period of Spring, Summer, and early Autumn I had got to know and appreciate the mighty North and its hardy, hospitable and inventive people.!!!

The historic Bryggen at Bergen

CHAPTER 2

OTTA — LOM — SOGNDAL

Otta is a small friendly town on the Oslo–Andalsnes–Trondheim Railway in the Gudbrandsdal. Buses leave the station for the Rondane Mountains, Maloy on the west coast and Sogndal on the majestic Sogne Fjord.

Our route was westwards along a wooded valley beside the Vaga River. As the valley widened we passed larger farms. When we reached Lake Vaga the hillsides were flaxen with ripening rye and oats, for this is Norway's driest area. The bus followed the southern shore of the lake passing Garmo's fine old church.

As we reached Lom our friendly bus driver set us down at the hotel entrance. Fossheim hotel, run by the Garmo family is full of interest. The beauty of the mellow woodwork and the traditional furnishings was so relaxing after an excellent dinner from the "open table". Among our fellow guests was a party of Norwegian geology students. Torgeir Garmo is a keen geologist whose writings on this subject are well known. Next morning, with their hammers, they were off early for a long walk.

We visited the hotel's own geological museum, and the fine Stave church Norway's largest, before continuing to Sogndal. The road followed the rushing river to Elveseter, a photographer's delight, and through the splendid Boverdalen climbing steadily towards the distant peaks. At Bovertun and later Krossbu several keen walkers alighted. To the left lay the snow-capped Galdhopiggen, Norway's highest mountain and the whole everchanging panorama was awe-inspiring as we drove on to Sognefjell with its splendid glacier views.

Before we began to descend to Turtago we noticed by the roadside that intriguing phenomenon "red snow", caused by algae that live in long standing snow, which has been compressed. A multitude of splendid vistas, including the rugged peaks of the Skagastolstindene were enjoyed and at Turtago there was still high mountain vegetation. Descending we passed through several floral zones until reaching the Fortun valley, with the lovely small white "new church". We saw the site of the original Stave church, now at Fantoft in Bergen.

Soon afterwards we reached Skjolden and the view of the Luster Fjord from our hotel was breathtaking.

Next morning we joined the early bus to drive by the Luster Fjord through Dale, where the stone church has a rich, fascinating interior, and Gaupne with its historic wooden church. Shortly after passing the turning to the Nigard glacier the bus made a brief halt at the Torvis Fjord Hotel.

Herr and Fru Bugge Naess were bidding farewell to some guests and having seen their cordial hospitality decided to stay there sometime later.

The journey from Marifjora to Sogndal is very scenic through fertile farmlands, forests, lakes, and rushing rivers. At Solvorn we could see across the fjord the Urnes Stav Kirke, the oldest standing. Sogndal, by the fjord shore is a fine, busy shopping and communication centre.

* * * * * *

We did return to Marifjora and had a highly enjoyable time. From this quiet fjord hotel with ample food and comfort we learnt much about the nature and history. Kjell Naess, the brother of Per Bugge Naess took us on several excursions in the hotel bus and by boat.

VOSS TO SOGNDAL

On leaving Voss our bus drove by beautiful lakes and the famous Tvindefoss to Vinje. It was blossom time and the lace-capped Hegg trees were at their best. Soon the road began to climb past scattered farms each with its red barn and meadows bright with dandelions. Before long these gave way to more rugged scenery with tumbling streams cascading down the hillsides.

We felt in another world as the bus sped between high banks of hard packed snow across the Vikafjell. Skiers and sunbathers were enjoying the snow and sun in the warmth of the direct and reflected rays.

The ice on the mountain lakes was just beginning to give. At our next halt, as we stood on the snow, we gazed far into the valley to a blue lake amid green pastures and beyond to more snow-capped mountains. How different was this compared with last summer when the only white in sight was the far distant Jostedal Glacier, Europe's largest.

We began descending and Vik lay spread below us beside the Sogne Fjord. Lower and lower we twisted and there to our left was the tiny Hopperstad Stave Church atop a hillock flanked by richly-hued copper beaches.

The road levelled out as we drove to the fjord's edge and along it past blossoming orchards to Vangsnes to board the ferry. Having crossed to the north shore we continued along it from Hella through Leikanger to Sogndal.

The beauty and serenity of the Sogne Fjord that May morning is unforgettable

The serene beauty of Vangsvatnet at Voss

BALESTRAND—A tourist paradise on the Sogne Fjord.

CHAPTER 3

THE ROAD TO NORTHERN FINLAND

My most enjoyable journey to Finland was during the middle of Summer. I left Sweden at the beginning of the Midsummer celebrations, and hitch-hiked first to Tampere, Finland's second largest city. As this was my third trip I felt thoroughly at home amongst the friendly Finnish inhabitants, for by now I knew they would always give a helping hand to anyone if proved necessary. Tampere is one of my favourite towns in Finland, and although it has the largest factories in the whole of Finland, it also is surrounded by lakes and woods. Tampere is truly called "The Manchester of the North" as it specialises in textiles and clothing, and yet has some delightful parks right in the very centre of the town. The town is the sole possessor of an Institute of Journalists and its Institute of Social Sciences can boast of a capacity of 6,000 students.

At the new youth hostel I was amazed to not only find a bright snack-bar with delicious food, but also a swimming pool and sauna bath. After a hot shower I took a long stroll through the town and visited the Russian Orthodox Church. Finland is the only Nordic land which supports this faith, as the majority of Scandinavians are Lutherian. It was a splendid feeling to look at the dedicated paintings by talented Russian painters. I was fascinated by the great quantity of Ikons, carvings and murals housed under one roof. I also visited the world-famous open-air theatre, the most unique in Finland, at is has a revolving auditorium.

Well rested and relaxed, I left the following day towards Jyvaskyla, and although the going was rather slow, I found the shade of the pine trees a great help, as the weather had suddenly become very hot and humid. Seldom have I seen such magnificent specimens of trees, growing right to the road's edge as far as the eye could see, their scent was fresh and fragrant, and it brought back schoolboy recollections, when I first found a fascination for trees.!! Trees form a priceless contribution to mankind's well-being, both now and in the future, and by careful planting they have reclaimed deserts, as in North Africa, Israel, and the Russian Steppes. And in the giant Redwood forests of California and Oregon, many of the forests date back before Christ and the Greek and Roman Empires. We may invent substitutes, but trees will always form a happy link in our everyday happiness and prosperity. Soil conservation, and proper control of floods and drought depends largely on how we respect our faithful friends, the trees.!!

By the late afternoon I reached Jyvaskyla, heavy rain and intermittent thunder had left a delightful freshness in the atmosphere. Here I ate a hearty meal, and waited three hours for the night-train eastwards, as I had always longed to see the glorious beauty of the Finnish landscape during the long Summer twilight nights, and experience the midsummer celebrations.

Jyvaskyla, with a population of nearly 60,000 is a rapidly expanding industrial centre. It is in the heart of Finland's most productive forested area. At nearby Vaajakoski millions of logs are floated down to the mills for sorting, before being processed into wood pulp, paper and various other forest products. The town was the first to establish the first elementary schools and teachers training college giving instructions in Finnish. Each year an important art and music festival is held in Jyvasklya, and I saw some of this on my return journey.

This night journey was so moving and quietly beautiful that I shall always remember it for many years to come. The slow train crossed many small bridges, and the calm waters of the lakes mirrowed the reflections of the slender birches and dark firs at the edges of the shores. The Finns were also celebrating Midsummer, and everywhere stood farming families beside their blazing bonfires, how happy they looked.!! The sky was clear with a few high clouds reflecting the rays of the slowly setting sun, while whisps of mist hung near the water's edge. The silence was so complete, even at Midnight the light hardly faded. Early in the morning the forest slowly awakened, and the initial faint calls of birds turned into a loud and lovely song.!!

The train arrived at Joensuu, a small town quite near the Soviet frontier, it had no platform and compared with other stations seemed somewhat primitive. The vast forests of North Karelia came to the very outskirts of the town, and near the station was even a small farm with a few cows grazing contently. I hitch-hiked north, but the going was slow, and the long night's journey made me feel tired. Everywhere were endless forests, and a maze of lakes. I noticed that on the scattered farms there were no fruit trees, as the growing season was too short, and early and late frosts were very frequent. The farmers grew red and blackcurrants, as this fruit matured very quickly. By the late afternoon I arrived at the village of Nurmes, it seemed like a scene from a wild west film, the cottages and wooden houses bordered rough, unsurfaced streets, and the surrounding hills were densely wooded. I found a vacant room at a small Christian guest house, nobody could speak English or Swedish, so I soon retired to my room and slept soundly for several hours. How delightfully fresh I felt as I once more set out on the open road, all my tiredness had vanished and the morning air was much fresher. It slowly became much warmer and after walking several miles between short lifts, I went to an isolated farm and asked for a drink of water. The farmers wife immediately asked me inside and insisted in giving me home-made rye bread and delicious coffee. I met her five children, the oldest boy was learning Swedish at school, he understood me very well, and was delighted when I gave him some Swedish postcards as I heartily thanked them and went on my way. The road through the forest was winding and narrow, in the ponds by the roadside were masses of tadpoles, and in the cracks in the road grew bright buttercups. Buttercups are the hardiest plants in the world, and are found high up in the mountains, well north of the Arctic Circle.

Swifts and swallows flew effortlessly overhead, how wonderful it was to see such an abundance of life, as far North as Greenland and the perma-frost region of Siberia and Canada. Here the growing season is extremely short, from the middle of May until early September. The farmers wage an eternal struggle with nature, and a freak Summer frost near the end of August can play havoc with their crops. Much of the rugged terrain was swampy, so there was an abundance of insect life, dragonflies flew across the deserted road, and butterflies were prolific. I walked on and on, waiting for a passing car, but only about one car passed by after almost waiting two hours.

I became quite desperate, especially as there was no sign of human habitation to be seen anywhere. Suddenly I noticed a forest worker wearing old, torn clothing, on a very old cycle. I tried to make him understand my plight by pointing at the road and also at my watch, he seemed to understand and vanished from my sight. How lonely I felt, but after waiting about twenty minutes, he just as suddenly reappeared, this time with his son, also riding a cycle. The son joined me, I rode his Father's cycle, and after a short time, we came to a road junction, and he waved Goodbye. And after all this kindly help from this true Finnish friend I was able to proceed on my way and by the evening I arrived in Kajaani a small but attractive town situated near the banks of two rapids. The Finnish poet, Elias Lonnrot, lived here for some time while he composed the national epics, Kalevala and Kantelar. The youth hostel was also used as a school for most of the year, small and homely, and I lost no time in having a hot shower which proved very refreshing.

Tellervo, the young lady who was the warden, spoke perfect English she had worked in California and London, and was divorced from her Swedish husband. Her son, Tommy, was very intelligent for his mere five years and seemed to delight in asking ceaseless questions. I liked the town, and as a brief respite from the long travel, decided to spend another day there. Tellervo's parents invited me to their home, and Tommy insisted in showing me his toys and making me join in a few games. Her parents were extremely interested, as it was seldom an Englishman ever came to this remote, Northern town. Her Father had worked at the meteorological station at Sodankyla, and related his experiences in Arctic Lapland.

Kajaani is only 150 miles south of the Arctic Circle, yet the short Summers enable the parks to display fine pine and birch trees. Many vegetables are delivered from further south, as they cannot mature in the very short growing period. I noticed that particularly in Northern Finland the people are often rather short, partly due to a diet often lacking in fresh dairy products, and fresh fruit and vegetables, all of which contribute greatly to healthy growth. I headed once more in a northerly direction, and here my progress was also very slow. About noon I reached Suomussalmi, near here a fierce battle between Russians and Finns took place in World War 2. I viewed the modern Finnish Church, I rather liked its mixture of wood and concrete and sense of harmony and inspiration of its architect. Outside were the simple graves of many fine young Finnish soldiers, most of them had been killed in their early twenties.

And already this tragic period of Finnish history is past, and instead friendship, commerce, and cultural, relations are increasing with the Soviet Union. Finland has a stable policy of strict neutrality and this does much towards East-West peace.

The journey North from Suomussalmi was even more wild and remote, and the going just as slow. I noticed that firs had become the predominant trees they looked so strange with their long tapering stems and thin, narrow branches. Many of the trees, especially the birches, had split trunks, caused by the rapid expansion after a sudden thaw. The heat was very exhausting, and as I passed a lonely lake, I suddenly had the impulse to take a swim. But even as I went into the water some mosquitoes followed me, and when I emerged, they were even more bloodthirsty. As I hastily dressed, I did my best to keep them at bay, but they still kept on biting. Only after a quick sprint was I at last able to evade their attention.

For several miles I walked wearily on, and as evening came, was still far from the nearest village. And once again a swarm of hungry mosquitoes came into the attack, and as fast as I killed a few, others alighted on my perspiring skin. How I cursed them, and became extremely tired and angry with this frustrating situation. At long last a passing farmer slowed down, he was quietly laughing, and offered me a lift, much to my consolation. Luckily he could speak Swedish, and drove me to the nearest village of Peranka. At the village cross-roads was a cafe, it was a room inside a farmhouse, and here I drank some very strong coffee and home-made cake, and began to relax.

At the farm was an adjoining sauna-house, and I was invited to take a Sauna bath. The Sauna is the true symbol of Finnish hospitality and I gratefully accepted their kindness.!! The wooden hut was heated by a blazing log fire, over which was a small platform with pebbles. I and two other Finns splashed water on the pebbles from time to time, and this created a hot, steamy atmosphere. The heat was so intense I gasped for breath, but how wonderful it was to perspire so freely, it was a tonic beyond compare for my tired limbs, and I felt so clean and fresh as I emerged into the open. Now I fully realised how the Finns adore the Sauna as something almost sacred.!!

There was no vacant room at the farm, so I was obliged to spend the night of perpetual daylight in the Sauna hut. It was impossible to sleep on the hard wooden benches, and I had to keep all the windows closed to keep out the mosquitoes. At half past eleven the sun slowly sank below the forested horizon, and an hour later it was shining merrily away. How I envied those fortunate beings who were sound asleep in a comfortable bed.!! In the early morning the forest birds twittered, I was surprised how much noise there was in the Northern forest.!!

I took an early morning stroll, everywhere was completely deserted, I had a strange feeling at being at one with the universe and the stress and strain of modern civilisation seemed far remote. Amongst the rolling hills roam deer, wolves, ermine, otters and even brown bears. Here, in this northern region, one can sense the still prevalent old pioneer spirit, something which brings out the best in every single man who has finer feelings in his outlook on life.!! When I returned to the farm, the cheerful farmer gave me a simple breakfast of black rye bread, jam, milk, and black strong coffee. His wife, and two teenage daughters, Kirstii and Maija, joined me. The girls were short and very blond, and as they had been learning Swedish at school, they were able to converse with their full interest and they also asked me to write to them. Then they commenced work, and milked the cows, which were much shorter than those living in warmer climes. How sorry I felt for the cows and the tethered goats, as they were continually plagued by a swarm of flies I helped weed a vegetable plot which grew a few potatoes, radishes, lettuce, and carrots.

Later a solitary car stopped and after such a long wait it seemed too good to be true.!! The driver was very charming, and pointed to the wonderful vistas of the dark green forests, high hills, and lakes glittering like jewels in the sun. We used one or two ferries to cross some of the lakes. Made of wood, they looked rather primitive, but they served their purpose. During the winter the ice became so thick that vehicles could be driven straight over the frozen lakes. The road wound through the narrow valleys surrounded by thickly forested hills, passing over wooden bridges over ravines and rushing streams. It was so warm that I kept on dozing off to sleep, in fact, had there been a bed in the car, I would have slept soundly the whole of the journey.

At the village of Taivakoski I thanked the driver for his help, it had a small timber mill and was a rail terminus, chiefly used for transporting timber products to the port of Kemi or Oulv on the Gulf of Bothnia. Luck was with me, and only after a few minutes a passing lorry stopped. The driver was transporting a small hay cutting machine to the community of Kuusamo, my final destination. It was a very lonely road, with an almost clear view for one or two miles, with stunted fir and birch trees on either side of the road. It was just like a setting from the wild tundra of Siberia or Northern Canada, mile after mile of desolate rocky hills and trees, many of them twisted and scarred by the harsh climate, and no sign of human habitation.

As the lorry passed over the brow of a hill I caught my first glimpse of Kuusamo, how tiny this Arctic settlement seemed in the distance. Once the settlement was reached, I lost no time in reaching the youth hostel, drank some lemonade and slept soundly for several hours., By early evening I awoke refreshed, and had time to see something of the Arctic village. The hostel was a school, and was annexed to a hospital. Both were heated from the same furnace, a great saving in fuel, as owing to the extreme climate, heating had to be more than adequate. How strange, now the sun was shining so warmly, and yet in the Winter the soil froze solid to a depth of three feet or over. The cost of heating, water drainage, and building is very high at these latitudes. Many small gardens grew marigolds, tagetes, lobelia, and hardy roses, most of the older houses were wooden, in sharp contrast to a few low blocks of concrete flats. Potatoes were the most popular vegetable, and did well provided not harmed by early frosts before the Autumn set in.

I noticed a small market gardener who grew cucumbers, tomatoes, lettuce, and flowers under greenhouses, and small children, were cycling around, wearing bathing costumes, as it was so warm. I sat down and watched the swifts and swallows flying gracefully over the church. The church was modern and light, with a concrete base and structure of wood, it radiated hope and good-cheer.!! Then I walked up to the observation tower on the top of the water reservoir, here I was well rewarded with a superb panorama. All around were the dark green forested slopes and "tunturi", rounded mountain fells with often sparce vegetation. To the east stretched a chain of lakes, which were partly in the domains of the Soviet Union.

To the north is the town of Rovaniemi, the centre of Finnish Lapland. It stands at the junction of the Ounasjoki and Kemijoki rivers, and was almost completely destroyed by the Germans in their retreat in World War 2. After years of determined hard work, it is a modern holiday resort and administration centre, with regular air and train communications from Helsinki.

And how well I slept that night of perpetual daylight, before returning to southern Finland and Sweden.

I left Kuusamo with a growing admiration and esteem for the Finnish people, and affection for this fascinating Land of Ten Thousand Lakes.

GUDBRANDSDALEN. RINGEBU STAVE CHURCH

Lake Loen, where Jostedalsbreen, Europe's largest glacier, forms an inspiring backdrop. Northern arms of this glacier are the Briksdal and Kjendal which may be visited from the Nordfjord, whilst from the Sogne fjord the southern arms, Boyum, Suphelle and Nygard may be approached quite easily.

CHAPTER 4

OSLO BERGEN AND NORWAYS MOUNTAINS

It was a clear September morning, the air was fresh and invigorating, the sky a deep blue, and the trees glistening with heavy dew. I had spent all the Summer working in the busy port of Gothenburg, and I felt sorry that I would not be gardening there until a later year. But Life is like a journey, time to say "Hallo" and also time to say "Goodbye". So many times I had lived at Stora Katrinelund youth hostel, and watched the seasons slowly come and go, meeting people from all walks of Life.!! Aftet making some hot tea in the kitchen I carefully packed up my belongings in my rucksack, and thanked Signe, the Swedish American girl who who had worked most of the Summer at the reception.

As I walked through the busy streets, with the sun casting long shadows on the pavements and people hurrying to work, there was a feeling of light-hearted expectation and hope of a truly enjoyable journey before me. I boarded a rather full tram, and as it crossed the bridge spanning the river Gota Alv, caught my last view of the harbourside. Soon I was at a busy crossroad where the northbound traffic along the west coast passed. I had not long to wait, before a small sports car stopped and a friendly young Swede offered me a lift. He was a great lover of Nature and the open-air life, and had recently returned from a highly enjoyable trip to Lapland. We passed the ancient castle at Kungalv, and were able to enjoy glimpses of the rugged coast and islands of the Swedish west coast. After about an hours journey the driver left along a side road, and I waited near a railway bridge, breathing the crisp Autumn air. I gazed at the surrounding landscape, of ripening hay, a mellow golden shade in the broad meadows of pale green, and pine forests stretching over the low hills, with overhead the blue turning into a gently purple just below the horizon. I had only been waiting a few minutes when suddenly a speeding car came to a halt and out jumped a tall, agile German. He seemed only too pleased to have some company, as he had been driving almost non-stop from Kiel. When we reached Uddevalla we stopped for a light breakfast at a cafe before continuing on our way.

How I enjoyed the journey, with the road winding amongst the thickly wooded hillsides, and a sky with delicate cloud formations to bless us on our way. About midday we crossed the Svinesund bridge and below the waters sparkled in the bright sunshine. And so we travelled on, this time on Norwegian soil, passing several small coastal towns and delightful, unspoilt villages. Towards the western horizon came the first glimpse of high mountains, and as we passed a large lake, we came to a sudden bend in the road. And a wonderful view greeted our happy eyes. Ahead was the Oslo Fjord, framed to the north and west by several mountain chains while directly ahead was Oslo, with some of its larger buildings plainly visible.

On the thickly wooded hillsides sloping down to the calm Oslo fjord were brightly painted Summer cottages and also stately homes with their large gardens and nearby pleasure boats. Passing the harbour, with its multitude of ships of every description, we slowed down near the Town Hall and I thanked the driver most heartily for his kindness. After a short walk through Karl Johansgatan, Oslo's main thoroughfare, I caught a tram to the hilly outskirts, and mounting a steep hillside, was at the Haraldsheim Youth Hostel. And how happy I was to meet many of my old friends.!!

Lars and his charming wife Hilde were very occupied with the reception, and Odd and Gertrud, with their two children, Gunnar and Elizabeth made me welcome. I telephoned Margit, and in the evening, my blond Norwegian friend called and we drove up to the wooded hills surrounding Oslo. We dined at a small restaurant and spent an enjoyable hour talking about the events of the past Summer, it was in Gothenburg we formed our friendship.

The hostel were short of staff on a Sunday, so I was able to spare some of my time on Sunday morning helping them with a few odd jobs. At lunch time Margit called and we drove along a fine road, which skirted the suburbs of the town, and following the shores of the Oslo fjord for some time. Then came a gradual long ascent up into the mountains, and the route passed the quiet waters of Lake Tyrifjord. At the small town of Honefoss we stopped for some light refreshments before resuming our journey. The high mountains, partly covered by thick, slowly moving clouds, and the lower slopes with their thickly forested cover had a strange fascination of their own. The trees often grew with their branches overhanging the narrow, winding road, and the deep lakes reflected the shapes of the tall pines with the mountains in the background.

Now and then rain clouds darkened the Autumn skies, but this did not change the inspiring majesty of the Norwegian landscape in its everchanging moods. I realised how much the citizens of the big European cities missed, and the falseness of the "Status Symbol", especially by so-called successful business men. For a financial gain is often a spiritual loss, and the best things in Life are free, to be gained by quiet contemplation or well-earned effort. Little wonder that Grieg and Ibsen were so strongly influenced and inspired by the Norwegian Nature which gave them lasting joy, inward contentment, and joyous harmony in their daily lives. Mountains cover the greater part of Norway, much of the land is forested, while only a small part is under cultivation. On the rivers timber floated slowly down to the paper mills at Honefoss, while on the farms there were piles of neatly stacked tree trunks which had been recently felled.

Many goats and sheep grazed on the sloping meadows, and many of the farms were painted in a most inviting manner. Goats are one of the hardiest animals in the world, and can live amongst sparse vegetation.

LOEN – Where beauty surrounds one in perfect harmony.

Still morning scene on Trondheim's Nidda River. R.P.

Near Honefoss, where the land sloped gently south and was protected by mountains from the north and east, grew some of the most extensive orchards in the whole of Norway and the ripe fruit and Autumn tints on the leaves was an impressive sight. I seemed almost sad as we approached Oslo and the peace and beauty of the mountains were left behind. We made a halt by the harbourside, quite near the Town Hall and watched the people and traffic pass by.

On the radio we heard about the passing of Albert Schweitzer, and I felt deeply moved as I listened to a Norwegian talking about his ideals, work, and belief, in a cultured, quiet voice. I realised more than ever what a gifted Idealist he had been.

Schweitzer always put his devotion to humanity far above easy pleasure and progress just for materialistic gain, seldom have individuals given their lives to such love and care for mankind in need.!! He came from a deeply musical family, his Father was a protestant pastor. As a youth he did all he could to learn about art and science, and by the age of thirty he was so able to devote his energies to serving humanity in the way he believed most fitting.

And so another day in that glorious land of forests, lakes, and mountains came to a sublime ending, as the sun slowly set below the western horizon, and the whole sky was transformed into a brilliance of colour.

Before leaving Norway I had the pleasure of working several days at Haraldsheim, and preparing the garden for the Autumn. And what a pleasure it was to work all day with splendid views over Oslo, the fjiord, the nearby thickly wooded hills, and the mountains in the background. As time passed, so did the beauty of the landscape change, not only daily, but also from hour to hour. I could wake up with the bright sun making it a sheer joy to be alive, sometimes the day would be rather rainy and dull, and so often the evening would be clear in a magical way, so that the lights of the city would shine far and wide and could be seen for a distance of many miles. Often the warden's children would join me in the garden, Gunnar and Elizabeth would ask questions, sometimes just for fun, but often out of sincere interest, and children all over the world have so much in common. How I love the spontaneous and open ways of small children, we can learn much from their simplicity. When I had finished my work I looked forward so much to returning to England and my dear Mother.

I felt sadly reluctant at leaving Oslo, but I decided to use the opportunity to travel to Norway's west coast and experience some magnificent scenery on the way. Several cars gave me short lifts, and a long distance was covered on foot, in the winding Hallingdal valley. Sometimes I joined in friendly conversation with a farmer, or relaxed on a grassy verge admiring the scenery. A Danish family drove me several miles, how overjoyed they were to see the mountains, so different to the smiling fields of agricultural Denmark.

As I watched a divine sunset, the outlines of distant peaks stood out sharply against the crimson horizon. Slowly the brightness of the glowing sky faded, and the green meadows and forested slopes took on deeper hues as until it was completely dark. Gol was my night's destination, a delightful mountain centre, with numerous hotels and homely guest houses. The youth hostel warden was rather plump and very jovial and made me feel immediately at home. A restaurant was also in a small annexe to the hostel, but I felt far too tired to eat much.

The night was bitterly cold, and overhead the stars shone in a strength and fascination of the splendour of Christmas, and it was so silent. Indeed, it was so silent that I could hear a train two or three miles away. And when I awoke, the house tops, trees, and fences were sparkling with a delicate frost. I walked slowly from the hostel, and as the mountain road was reached, the sun slowly rose, and the first rays turned the whiteness of the frost into a dazzling crimson. For several miles I walked by the side of a swiftly flowing river, and as the last houses of Gol were passed, civilisation seemed so distant. The intense stillness was broken only by the faint distant tinkle of cow bells and I breathed the fragrant scent of the lofty pine trees. Sometimes I could hear the water pounding against gigantic boulders as the road came much closer to the swiftly flowing river. Here was peace beyond all understanding, where one found strong resources of radiant faith and greater knowledge of the finer sides of life. And is not sentiment and appreciation of beauty a priceless asset which can ennoble our everyday lives in many aspects. And I only wished I could have stayed longer in this mountain terrain before returning home.

A passing lorry rumbled to a halt along the dusty, narrow road, and the smiling driver, who was working on a hydro-electric scheme, gave me a seat. He pointed to the mountain where he worked, explaining how the water travelled several miles through a narrow tunnel from a remote lake before reaching the huge turbines, and often the tunnels were several miles long.

Today Norway is the most important supplier of hydro-electric power in the whole of Western Europe, and even the remotest hamlet is supplied with electricty. The electro-chemical and electro-metallurgical industries form a highly helpful part of Norwegian progress and give work to many in formerly backward regions. I was offered yet another lift in an old lorry, and how happy I was to be at the large community of Al in Hallingdal. This small route centre has a large proportion of its inhabitants working for the Norwegian railway, and when steam was the main source of power the passengers changed trains before proceeding to more mountainous terrain on their journey over the high Hardanger plateau.

At the local school the children gave me a hearty welcome, a year before I gave them some lessons in English and Geography, as I took a liking to the school when I passed by. I greatly enjoyed speaking to them

BERGEN – City with a special charm and atmosphere.

Kjosfossen cascades beside the Flam line.

about my travels, and afterwards I was invited to the home of a Norwegian couple. Esther taught English, and her husband taught woodwork and metalwork. Their home was built from timber, and I felt very much at home in its homely and warm atmosphere. Esther was for some time a refugee in Sweden, and found the Swedes very helpful and kind, even though rather reserved at first. Her Father was a seaman's pastor, and was at present working at Narvik, in North Norway. Over a delicious meal we joined in a lengthy conversation. Towards the evening they drove me in their old faithful English car to the station, and as the train moved out, we waved each other Goodbye. Relaxed and contented after the splendid meal, it was a joy to travel on the Oslo—Bergen Line, a masterpiece of engineering.

Norway has 2,700 miles of railway, and about half of this has already been electrified. The sparce population and high cost of maintainence still makes many of the lines run at a loss, especially during the Winter, but in the south and east, the Ostfold and Westfold near Oslo, they run at a profit. Just in this journey of 300 miles, the Oslo—Bergen Line has no fewer than 181, tunnel's which have a total length of 30 miles. After the thickly forested valley of Hallingdal was passed, the train slowly climbed higher and higher, passing quiet blue lakes, high waterfalls, and rushing mountain streams, their waters blue green, as they were of glacial origin. Only birch trees, stunted with the cold, grew here, and higher up mosses, lichens, and few bushes survived. Finse, the highest station, well over 4,000 feet was reached, and all around glistened the mighty glaciers of the Hardanger Plateau. It was here where Scott of the Antarctic trained for his expedition to the South Pole.

Moving still westward, the train traversed many long wooden tunnels, erected for protection against the huge falls of snow during the long Winter months. Passing Myrdal, it was so impressive to see the reappearance of the first thickets of birch trees, with here and there a solitary pine, and the lower slopes were thickly forested with tall pine woods, a purple green colour in the approaching twilight. Cows grazed in the isolated meadows, how peaceful it looked, just like a wonderful painting from the National Gallery in Oslo.! At the mountain resort of Voss the train made a lengthy halt, the station was full of almost frantic activity, tourists alighting, porters carrying heavy baggage, and buses and lorries coming and going. By late evening Bergen was reached, what a comparison it was to see the multitude of lights gleaming brightly in the cool September night.!! A strong breeze was blowing as I caught the bus from the station to the Montana Youth Hostel, and from the mountainside I had an extensive view over the town Bergen is the birthplace of Grieg and Ludvig Holberg, how fortunate they were to live in surroundings which gave them imagination and inspiration.!! Each year Bergen celebrates with a music festival, and thousands of tourists from many nations come to join in the celebrations.

It is the peace, majesty, and unending fascination of the fjords which attract tourists. Several of the fjords are long and winding, such as the Sogne and Hardanger fjords, penetrating as far as a hundred miles from the open sea. For anyone who has time, the Geiranger fjord should not be missed.!! Each turn of the steeply sloping fjord opens up to new vistas of blue waters, small farms, meadows and woods, and above, high mountains their peaks capped by eternal snow.

While spending two pleasant days in Bergen, the time went all too quickly. Sometimes I would drink morning coffee in a cosy cafe close to the fish market, and watch with fascination the people buying vegetables, flowers, and fish, almost as if time did not count to them, just the joy of restful pleasure of finding simplicity in their everyday lives.!! Bergen still retains many of her narrow, cobbled streets, old wooden houses often dating back to the Hanseatic era. when Bergen did a lively trade with Lubeck, Hamburg, and Bremen. For almost a whole day a continuous rain set in, and so I spent several hours in the City Library, reading English books and weekly magazines. I wrote about my Summer work and travel, and the local newspaper had it published.

How different it was, when the rain clouds slowly dispersed, and the warm bright sun turned the scene into one of gaiety and colour. And although Bergen is the second largest city in Norway, its surroundings have a highly varied and stimulating beauty. Thanks to the warming influence of the Gulf Stream, the mild climate allows beech, oak, and chestnut trees to grow equally as well as in the British Isles. And from Bergen the daily coastal boats depart for their long journey north to a multitude of ports, even as far away as Kirkenes, on the Soviet Frontier. So great is the length of Norway's coastline, that the extreme north-east is as far away as North Italy. These sturdy steamers are for many smaller coastal communities the only means of communication for most of the year.

Here one can rejoice in the natural beauty which surrounds us each turn we take.!! The countless thousands of simple visual scenes give us as much serene joy as the more spectacular ones. The smallest flower has the same perfection of beauty as the high forested mountains and starlit skies. And the wonder of the waterways in their magnificent sweep, the fine growth on the farms and forested hill give added incentive to the strong spirit of the Northern people.!! In Norway I have found that sentiment makes life richer and fuller in every meaning. Here one can find strength and solace amongst the vastness of the Finnish forests, the rolling landscape of Sweden, and the sublime sunsets over Norway's lofty mountain peaks. So many of the "civilised" towns of Europe have the problems of industry and large towns, in Scandinavia one can still live in harmony with nature, both in the country and even the Capital cities. So life has few problems for the Northern peoples who live, work, play, and relax forever close to nature.!! And when I leave Bergen I always associate it with leaving Scandinavia until another happy, exciting, and fascinating year.!! I think of the beauty of the Northern Autumn which comes without failing, year after year, like a blessing divine. For Autumn comes slowly, lingering steeped in each lovely vista, before moving on slowly to another colourful scene. First is the far North, which rapidly changes into a splendour of brilliant gold and amber, while everywhere the tall pine and fir trees stand out darkly in contrast to the background of bright colours. The inland lakes, calm and silent, reflect the delicate hues of the sky and their brilliantly coloured surroundings.

In the Fjord country the Autumn comes slowly on the high meadows and forested slopes, showing more distinctly amongst the clearings of the small farmsteads. For here the maturing fruit and ripening hay turn the lower valleys into an everchanging patchwork of all shades of colour. Lastly, the parks and gardens of Bergen, Stavanger, and Oslo rejoice in their last show of Autumn tints before the first frosts descend. Besides every waterway the brilliantly arrayed trees bend gently over as though in admiration of their clearly reflected images. Even the small insignificant grasses and shrubs by the shores catch the light-hearted spirit and form an almost horizontal line to the colours of the forests which merge unto the bluish horizon. And although the days are shorter, they are still warm and delightfully clear, with long and calm twilights.

Yet no gifted and talented painter could portray every shade of colour so delicate and varied.!! And no equally brilliant actor could portray Autumn in all its slowly changing splendour.!! No wonder I feel sentimental when the time has come to sail from Bergen.!!

Here I bid Farewell to those heavenly Northern lands and their beloved peoples which have caught my ever-growing admiration and fascination.

The City hall in Stockholm, where sky, sea, and land blend in perfect harmony.

ARCTIC JOURNEY

CHAPTER 5

ARCTIC JOURNEY

One July morning I left the busy Oslo East Station on a Journey of great distance and immense interest and enjoyment. Soon the suburbs of this large city were far left behind, and the train travelled amongst broad fertile valleys and prosperous farms. Just north of Eidsvoll the train skirted Norway's longest lake, Mjosa, before making a lengthy halt at Hamar, a thriving market town with small industries. From here the route was due east to Elverum, with its many pulp and paper mills.

The region of the Osterdal was very wild, with only a few scattered farms, amidst huge forests of fir and pine. Here the busy, hectic life of Oslo seemed already long forgotten. The wide river Glomma flowed swiftly and silently past, its waters a clear blue, almost as blue as the bright Northern sky. The farms were subject to the severe frosts of the lengthy winters, so only a few hardy crops, such as oats, rye, and wheat were cultivated, and I watched the farmers busy with their haymaking. Only 90 years ago this remote region was opened up by the construction of the Roros railway, yet villages such as Rene and Koppang have hardly changed in population, and many of the smaller farms have become deserted.

Slowly the mountains on either side became higher and higher and the waters of the Glomma were swift and turbulent, pounding against the rocks and boulders as it sped on. Often I passed several miles before seeing any sigh of human habitation, and this region abounds in wild life. Foxes, elk, wolverines, even a few bears roam these vast tracts of forests, and how strongly I felt that we, like Peter Scott, should do all in our power to help and respect wild animals, many almost extinct. I managed to catch a fine view of Tronfjell mountain, over 5,000 feet, and after leaving Tynset, was on the threshold of the Roros Vidda, a bleak mountain plateau. The trees were rather stunted, and the atmosphere delightfully clear, bringing out the brightness of the colours in a most fascinating way.

At the old mining town of Roros I took a long stroll. This small copper mining centre was founded in 1644, and has a beautiful old stone church, a few stately mansions, and small, grey miners cottages. The latter resembled closely those of nearby Cornwall and parts of Wales. The writer, Johan Falkberget, depicted clearly the people of this isolated region, with an inborn knowledge of their hardships and struggles. A few miles away a few Lapps live with their herd of reindeer, amongst the moors, high fells and birch thickets. The train continued on its journey towards Trondheim, and followed the course of the winding river Gaula. I found a rapid descent of immense fascination, watching the river far below amongst deep ravines and lonely woods.

Lower land was reached, and I soon became engaged in conversation with some Norwegian railway workers, and was amazed at their knowledge of English. By the early evening I arrived in Trondheim, the ancient capital of Norway, and today the lively centre of the Trondelag region. How tired I was after the day's journey of 350 miles. I caught a local bus to the youth hostel, which was a fine modern building, sited on a steeply sloping hillside. A young student shared the same room as me, he was from the beautiful Sunnmore district of West Norway which I have twice visited.

Trondheim was formerly the capital of Norway, and was founded in 997 A.D. by the Viking King Olav Tryggvason, and today both Bergen and Trondheim are close rivals as to being the second largest cities in Norway, with populations close on 130 thousand I spent the late evening walking slowly round the older part of the town, near the lofty Nidaros cathedral, a highly important centre for Christian pilgrims in the Middle Ages. Indeed, it seemed as if time stood still, so carefully well preserved were all the buildings. I had true sentiment for the old, friendly wooden houses and the narrow cobbled streets still to be found. And I could most clearly visualise the sharp patter of horses hooves echoing along the streets and the prosperous merchants engaged in some business matter and having a friendly argument. What a story many of these ancient buildings could tell.!!

By the time I returned to the hostel I felt very tired and yet happy, and gave the warden's wife one of my books. The following morning I awoke fresh for another journey.!! I was fortunate to have a freindly chat with the warden, Rolf Kvam, he was a man of great statue, and even bigger charm and tolerant humour and intelligent understanding. He refused any payment for breakfast as he had been reading my book the previous evening . As I set off for the station at a brief pace I noticed that many of the side streets were unpaved, in sharp contrast to Oslo. Ahead was a day's journey of 450 miles on the Nordland's Railway, a journey so spectacular and exhilarating that I shall never forget it. Only in 1962 was the line extended as far as Bodo, at immense effort and cost.

As the train left the station, it followed the coast very closely for several miles, and the surrounding smiling farmlands were so fertile and green, that for a moment I could have imagined it was somewhere in North Devon or Wales. Here, a mere 200 miles south of the Arctic Circle, beech trees, lilacs apples, and pears grow in abundance, thanks to the warming influence of the Gulf stream. As the town of Levanger was passed the landscape changed in a most sudden and unexpected way. The line ran inland, the farmsteads became scattered and ahead stretched ranges of mountains, their lower slopes covered with the deep green of coniferous forests, so similar to those of Central Finland and Sweden. As lake Snasvatn was sighted, the winding Namdal valley was entered. Each year many fishermen take their holidays here, it is also a paradise for those who love wild life and the solitude of unspoilt Nature.

JOTUNHEIMEN – the awe-inspiring SKAGASTOLTINDENE.

Trollhaugen, the home of Edvard Grieg in its peaceful setting near Bergen.

North of Majvatn the province of Nordland began. This province of sparce population short Summers, vast tracts of forests, swamplands, and high mountains with peaks often covered with eternal snow. I found endless delight as the train followed the narrow Vefsna valley, as the single track line crossed many high bridges and the pine and fir trees grew close to the track. At the town of Mosjoen, a lengthy halt was made, and I lost no time in drinking some extremely welcome coffee with some freshly made fruit cakes. The Aluminium works are very extensive and together with the local timber mills are highly productive. The closeness of the high mountains with their still unmelted patches of snow gave this town a rather bleak atmosphere, as if Life in the Arctic was an eternal struggle.

I became very friendly with a young American, a teacher by profession, who also taught Norwegian to some of his students in America.

The next town of importance was Mo in Rana, it has grown very rapidly in the last few years, thanks to its extensive iron and steel works which were established in 1955, and most of the town's population of 25,000 is dependant on this industry. As most of the houses have only been recently constructed, and most of the streets are still unpaved, the town possesses something of the pioneer spirit.

Then began the journey through the winding Dunderland valley, there was very little trace of human habitation as the train winded upwards along the side of the swiftly flowing river Rana. The lower mountain slopes were covered with the dark green forests of slender firs, giving a most weird effect. As the train slowly reached the lower slopes of the Saltfjell mountain plateau, the trees grew scarcer until they completely disappeared. I could see sometimes small groups of stones, here the Lapps once worshiped and made sacrifices to their gods. As the Arctic Circle was reached, the train moved at a slower pace, and on each side of the track stones had been erected to mark the exact location of the Arctic Circle.

Magnificent vistas of windswept mountains and deserted valleys had a strange fascination and grandeur. This immense and vast beauty of the landscape was almost impossible to describe. The high mountain peaks and steep slopes took on everchanging shades of colour as the clouds, floating swiftly past in the high wind, left their fleeting shadows on the rocky, moss grown slopes. Nowhere was any sign of habitation to be seen, and these precious moments brought a feeling of delightful exhiliration and fulfilment.!!

On the train was a delightful hostess from Trondheim called Vera, and she presented us with a certificate which stated that we had passed the Arctic Circle by train. As we approached the entrance to the Lonsdal Valley, a few dwarf birches and here and there a single stunted pine tree made a welcome contrast to the vast wilderness. Nearby was the moraine valley of the Junkerdalsaura, and here can be found plants which date back to the Ice Age, and only in Spitsbergen can be found similar plants At Rognan, a station quite close to the sea, on Saltdal fjord, the change was amazing, for here were smiling meadows with fragrant new-mowed hay, and hardy crops such as oats and barley did well. The farmsteads, with their brightly painted wooden houses and neat fences with nearby piles of freshly cut timber looked so friendly and inviting.

At Fauske the train turned westwards in the direction of Bodo, and to the south the snow-capped peaks of the Borvasstindene mountain range glistened in the bright rays of the late evening sunshine. Between Bodo and the hinterland, where the Saltdal and Skerstad fjords meet, is the Saltstraumen strait, where 655 million cubic meters of water rush through 4 times daily.

This day's journey took 13 hours and when the train reached Bodo I felt so tired that I felt almost lethargic as I walked along the wide streets in the chilly air. A wonderful transformation has been made in the last few years, with modern buildings and an ultra-modern civic centre. Bodo is an important air, rail, and road centre, and a thriving fishing port, thanks to its closeness to the Lofoten islands and the fishing grounds. I met the American for a short time, and, feeling very hungry, went to the nearest snack bar for a meal.

That night it was almost impossible to sleep, as apart from the eternal light, lorries would sometimes rumble past on the unsurfaced road nearby. However, it was delightful getting up early in the morning and watching the fishing smacks chugging along the calm waters under a sky so blue. I caught the early train to Fauske, before joining the regular bus to Narvik.

Never have I been on such a heavily laden bus, it was almost as if we were on some Arctic expedition, farming families and local tradesmen were the chief occupants, and at the back of the bus was a large pile of luggage heaped waist high. One could fully realise the inhabitants led rather a hard life, one or two were quite short, and were probably of Lapp extraction. We passed the low surroundings of the Fauske marshes with their abundant bird life, and on reaching the Sorfolla fjord, caught a ferry at Sommersett Bonasjoen. Formerly the ferry sailed from Rosvik, a trading centre founded over 200 years ago. Climbing on up a fairly steep incline the high mountain pass of Tennvatn rewarded us a superb view of seven lakes. Further on the village of Krakmo was passed, here the poet and writer Knot Hansum lived at a farm and wrote his best known works, "Segelfoss Town" and "Growth of the Soil".

As the bus, high up amongst the wild mountains, began a steady descent, I was rewarded with a splendid view of the glistening snow of the numerous peaks of the Lofoten islands, and the nearby Vestfjord. Although a good distance away, the atmosphere was so clear that the grandeur of the scene was even more wonderful. Crossing from Bognes to Skarberget by another ferry, I gazed upwards to the high mountains which sloped sometimes almost vertically into the deep waters. Stetind, rising steeply on all sides, is renown as being the finest natural obelisk in the World. Nearby is the narrowest point of Norway, and at the head of the Tysfjord, it is only 5 miles to the Swedish border.

As we drove amongst the mountains between Eford and Tysfjord the rock formations were most peculiar, as rushing water and extreme frost had polished them completely bare in places. Yet in the valleys near the coast the farms, with their flocks of sheep and cattle looked fairly prosperous, and the birch and pine trees grew extremely well. After taking two more ferries, the outskirts of Narvik were reached, it was late July, and the lilacs and tulips were only just in bloom, as the Summer had come later than usual. Majestic birches flanked the well paved road, and the low evening sun shone on calm, blue waters, while to the west rose a multitude of islands, some with snow on their highest points.

Thanks to the mild influence of the Gulf Stream, Narvik, almost a thousand miles north from Oslo, is ice-free all the year round, in sharp contrast to the ports of Finland and Sweden, on the Gulf of Bothnia, which are often ice-bound for months. The harbour has very extensive loading docks, handling annually million of tons of Swedish iron ore which is transported by train from the mining centre of Kiruna. After alighting from the bus, I walked up the steep hill to the youth hostel, but felt very despondent when told that they were packed to the limit with tourists. So I returned to the railway station, and was fortunate enough to find a suitable address for the night. A kindly old lady gave me a small room for the night, she also gave me some supper, and refused to take any money.

When I awoke the following morning, I noticed, amongst several books on a shelf, a magazine with a long article on the humanitarian and idealist Albert Schweitzer. In 1952, while visiting Oslo, he was awarded the Nobel Peace Prize for his outstanding work for humanity, and was given a very moving and delightful reception by the freedom-loving Norwegians. And although I am not very religious, I was deeply moved by the article about that fine Idealist.!! His aspirations and belief means so much in this war-torn World, and the stress and strain of modern civilisation.

I caught the early train which travels the entire journey to Stockholm, a distance of a thousand miles, in only a day.!!

This Ofoten Line carries the iron ore from Sweden, and as the line only has a single track, the long, heavily loaded trains are controlled by remote control as they are shunted into the sidings. For some distance the line followed the southern edge of the Rombak fjord, before making a much steeper climb up into the surrounding mountains, through several tunnels, and past many cuttings and over high bridges, the views were very impressive. At Straumes, about four miles from Narvik, was a small station, and here was a tiny village and the last hillside farm before reaching the frontier. The Norddalsbrua bridge offered a last splendid vista of the Rombaksbotn region, and the trees became stunted as we passed the last Norwegian station at Bjornfjell.

Now I was filled with a wonderful feeling of anticipation of the forthcoming journey as the train neared Vassijaure, on the Swedish frontier. At this frontier station, the land was very rocky and barren, with very little soil, and yet a few dwarf birches grew amongst the patches of still unmelted snow. What a wonder it was to see them growing so far north, and 2 thousand feet above sea level. I noticed one or two window boxes of flowers at the home of the station master, he certainly was a true lover of flowers and warm colours.!! And so I was in Swedish Lapland, a vast and wild land of swamps, uninhabited mountains, and forests of pine, fir, and birch trees. Much of Swedish Lapland is still a virgin wilderness and has some of the best wild-life national parks in the whole of Europe. This is the region of extremely marked contrasts, long cold Winters, short warm Summers, Autumns of indescribable colour and beauty, and a Spring which comes almost like a great explosion, growth taking place immediately after the snow melts under the warm rays of the sun which never sets for many weeks.

How fascinating it was, looking up at the ranges of high mountains on the Swedish frontier, with eternal snow on their lofty summits, mosses and lichens on their steep rocky slopes, and below swift turrents which had made deep ravines into the rocks over the passage of time. Slowly we reached lower terrain, and for a long time we followed the shores of the Lake Tornetrask, and to the North I could see the mountains which pass across the frontiers of Norway, Sweden, and Finland. And I noticed a small Lapp settlement by the side of a small lake, smoke was rising from a wooden shack vertically into a cloudless sky. Many of the Lapps are no longer nomadic wanderers, and live happily together in small communities, near the rivers and lakes, where fishing is good.

There are about 7,000 Lapps, most of them live in Scandinavia, and also in the Kola Peninsular, in the Soviet Union. About a quarter of the Lapps are occupied with reindeer, which number about 200,000, far more than the human inhabitants of this vast region. The Lapps are short and stocky, with spontaneous humour, industrious, and today often well educated. Some of them even grow a few potatoes, rye, and oats. And as most of them live a long way from towns, they make it quite an occasion when they make a trip to civilisation. Here they purvey large stocks of food and essentials, attend a funeral or marriage, or even legal action.

For the Lapps, the reindeer is the most important means of livelihood, warm clothing, meat and fresh milk. Each winter the herds are rounded up into compounds, to be sorted for their special requirements. This is the season of great festivity, as the Lapps wearing their brightly coloured costumes, swirl their lassoes in the air as they run quickly to and fro in a most energetic and determined manner. It reminds one of a wild-west setting, as the hooves of the kicking animals create a fine mist after hitting the dry, deep snow.

With their peaked caps, loosely worn jackets as an insulation against the cold, bright shoes of reindeer skin, and sometimes ornaments of pure gold or silver, they present a spirit of festivity. The shoes are pointed to enable them to be attached to the skis, and the jackets are full-skirted to prevent snow collecting and saturating the rest of their clothing.

This journey across Lapland was a few hundred miles, and most of the land was under coniferous forests. For even above the Arctic Circle trees manage to grow and mature well, for during the short but warm Summer, which lasts a brief 3 months, the growth is very rapid, thanks to the days without any length of darkness. Besides the track were small settlements with saw mills, often many miles apart in this northern wilderness.

Passing the iron-ore towns of Kiruna and Gellivare, it seemed an eternity before reaching Boden, a small but busy town and route centre not far from the Gulf of Bothnia. From here I went by a smaller train to Haparanda, over a hundred miles to the East, the most Eastern town in Sweden. Although I was very tired, the long walk to the Finnish frontier made a welcome break, and the warm evening sun helped me on my way. I crossed the Torniojoki river, this wide, slowly flowing stretch of water forms a natural frontier between Sweden and Finland. At Tornio the local tourist information gave me some helpful advice, the Finns were extremely helpful and did their best to help any stranger to their local neighbourhood.

Boarding a packed bus, I was immediately offered a seat by an alert young soldier, and it was not long before I was in Kemi, a busy and thriving industrial centre at the estuary of the Kemijoki river. I decided to stay here the night and made my way to a large restaurant where I enjoyed some excellent coffee. The whole youth of the town seemed to have collected there, how happy and carefree they were as they danced to some lively music. Much of the Finnish music is rather eastern in its character and resembles strongly that of the Russian and Hungarian music, especially the "Joika", which I find both unusual and fascinating.

I noticed that most of the buildings were very modern, for many towns were badly destroyed as the Germans retreated in 1944. Finland has for centuries experienced poverty, war, and hardships. She ceded after the war about twelve percent of her territory to the Soviet Union, including the eastern part of the province of Karelia, and the ice-free port of

Murmansk, her only port on the Arctic Sea. Finland was also forced to pay the huge sum of 80 million pounds of war reparations. And she paid on time, thanks to her honesty and dedicated industry.!!

When I reached the rather small and over crowded youth hostel, I found out that I was the sole Englishman there, most of the tourists were Americans, Frenchmen, and Germans. Sleep came with a delightful speed, before the dawning of another day. Awaking early, I strolled to the quiet outskirts of the town, and was given a lift to a large village further south. How relieved I was to find a station there, so bought a ticket to Kajaani, my last destination. The journey of about four hours was rather tedious, as none of the occupants spoke English or Swedish. But how overjoyed I was on reaching Kajaani, after a journey of 1,500 miles.!!

Most of the streets and buildings seemed familiar, although five years had elapsed since I was in Kajaani, and at the home of Tellervo's Mother I was made very welcome. Tellervo soon finished work, and with her son Tommy, joined us for tea. How wonderful it was to completely relax for a few days, I realised how much I needed the rest.

On my first day in Kajaani I visited the big timber and pulp factory which employs over 1,400 people of the town's 15,000 inhabitants. The manager, Von Zansen, made me welcome in his light, roomy office. He spoke fluent German and English, and his knowledge and capability, together with his sense of humour was a great tonic. Tellervo took two days off from work to show me something of the town and its precincts.

We made a trip by bus to Paltaniemi, a quiet, small village with an old, modest church which was built in 1726, it was made almost entirely of wood. Inside this friendly, mellow building were some splendid old paintings, showing clearly the dedication and skill of the workers who often took many years to complete their work. The Russian Czar Alexander stayed in a barn adjoining the Church, his horse-carriage and wooden boat were still carefully preserved. On the return journey we passed the airport which was in a small clearing in the forest. What a delightful setting, I thought, far more peaceful and unspoilt than most of the busy world airports.

The local paper gave an article about my travels, and the young reporter, Anne, was intelligent and industrious. Indeed, young or old, the Finnish woman of today is just as capable as any man, becoming architects, doctors, teachers and engineers. Finland was the very first nation to give women the vote, in 1906.

The few days rest and relaxation made the return journey even more enjoyable, it was good to be on the train once more and enjoy the Finnish Landscape. At Kontiomaki the train made a lengthy halt, the trees grew almost to the station. The forest was so thick and close, it

Morning splendour reflected on calm Olden Lake.

One smiling face of Old Bergen.

could well have been in some remote part of Canada, or in the heart of Siberia.

At Oulu I walked around for some time, and was able to more fully appreciate the fine progress being made in this rapidly growing major city. Oulu can be justly proud of having the most northerly university in the whole World, it was built in 1959. The town library has a splendid selection of books, for the Finns are some of Europe's biggest readers. Unfortunately fires have often devastated the older and more picturesque parts of the town, so the majority of the larger buildings are modern, and yet well built with vision and insight. Soon it was time to resume my journey, westwards to Sweden, at Haparanda it was so warm that I perspired freely and found a large portion of ice-cream more than welcome

The whole of the route was thickly forested, for several hundred miles, I changed trains at Boden, and by the late evening passed the Arctic Circle. The late train was almost empty, and the landscape wild and lonely, huge forests of pine and fir, which slowly, very slowly became slightly shorter as we moved north. The pines became less predominant, giving way to the slender fir trees and silver birches. I had a strange feeling of isolation, it was just as if the ordinary, everyday life was non-existant as the train sped on through the northern wilderness. How true was Dag Hammarskjold, who devoted his energies and ideals to World Peace and the United Nations, when he wrote the following in his diary. "He is one of those who has the wilderness for a pillow, and called a star his Brother. Alone—but loneliness can be a communion."

To the west of the small mining centre of Gallivare, I saw the wooded slopes of Mount Dundret. Here many festivities take place, including Sweden's most important alpine competition, the Lapland cup. The town has a very old church, given the name of "The Iron Ore Church". The church funds were collected by a well supported nation-wide contribution.

Near Gallivare is also a large Lapp community, and in this area the winters are extremely severe, as the land is fairly high and a great distance from the sea. Northwards the train sped, and the wildness and grandeur of the multitude of lakes and fast rivers and streams was beyond description. The immense tracts of forest seemed endless, I was completely surrounded by trees from every angle. But, slowly and surely, the tall pine trees gave way to a dominance of silver birches, and their graceful light beauty was reflected clearly in the still, blue lakes.

After what seemed an eternity I noticed a distant mountain which stood out distinctly above the endless forest. As it became larger and more distinct in shape, I recognised it as Kirunavaara mount, near Kiruna. This mountain is truly unique, for it possesses the biggest underground mine in the World. It is also a very important source of revenue for the Swedish industry, for the home market, and export of iron - ore, and steel products of high quality and durability. By the time the train reached Kiruna, it was nearly midnight, and yet I still felt mentally alert and receptive. The town had a rather wierd atmosphere, like somewhere in the Yukon or Northern Canada, I walked along the almost deserted streets, which were wide and flanked by birch trees on either side. After a long walk I arrived at the youth hostel, and I felt rather dispondent when told that it was closed, and nowhere could I find the warden. However, luck came my way, and two good-humoured Englishmen found me a place on the floor in a kitchen. The floor was far too hard to let me sleep, and some mosquitoes made it even worse, they kept on annoying me until the early hours of the morning. Still, I felt thankful, it was chilly and damp outside, and outside were even more bloodthirsty mosquitoes.

And I was well rewarded by a splendid sunrise, the first crimson rays of the sun caught the tops of the mountains, while the lower valleys were in various shades, and the remarkable contrast of colours was almost like a lunar landscape, as apart from the lower valleys, the mountain slopes were completely devoid of vegetation. Yet in the valleys was life in abundance. Dragonflies flew effortlessly nearby, swallows glided silently in the morning sky, and magpies strutted around in a dignified manner through the streets, in search of food. Here, in the Far North, Nature is active every single minute, making every opportunity to benefit from the brief Summer before the onset of the long Winter.

As I walked to the station, the heavy dew on the trees and shrubs glistened in the bright rays of the sun, and as I reached the town gardens on a hillside, the scent from the flowers and blossom on the shrubs was quite strong. On the top of this gently sloping hill was the town hall, it was modern, simple, and beautiful and resembled a typical Finnish building.

As I reached the station, I noticed a Lapp lady, who seemed very bright and humourous. I could tell she had a placid and gentle nature. She had a splendid Lapp dog, which took a great liking to me. I managed to find a few biscuits in my rucksack, and it ate them with speed and great relish. I felt quite reluctant to leave this fine specimen of animal, it seemed almost human and so understanding.

The restaurant in the station opened, and I was delighted on finding they had an open "Smargas table", with a wonderful variety of delicious food. I had such a good breakfast that it was just as if I had partaken in a sumptious banquet.

Soon I was amongst magnificent, rugged scenery, as the train followed the southern shores of Lake Tornetrask, which was partly obscured by light drizzle. As the rain clouds drifted slowly away, I had an unexpected view of the "Lapporten", where, from time immemorial, the Lapp nomads have wondered in their annual migrations from the East to the West, across the high mountain chain which separates Sweden from Norway. Westward the railway slowly climbed and as the terrain became higher, the mountain scenery was inspiring and had mile after mile of completely uninhabited areas. The remainder of the journey was rather uneventful, until I arrived in Trondheim, when I felt a great sense of unexpected joy.!!

Immediately I left the train in Trondheim, I had a delightful feeling of elation and inner peace, it was just like a wonderful homecoming. I had travelled well over a thousand miles non-stop since leaving Kajaani in Finland, and yet my tiredness disappeared as if by magic as I walked amongst the streets with people going to work who mingled with early morning shoppers who took life at a very unhurried pace. It was for me a return to civilisation. The roads and narrow streets were in a much better condition than those further north in Finland and Norway. And with a much larger population and buildings both greatly historic and carefully preserved, the town had a timeless atmosphere of harmony and steady progress.

The warden and his wife had read my book during my absence and made me feel completely at home. After the long journey and lack of regular exercise, I longed to return to do some useful work. So in no time I was busy in the garden, making the ground level for making a new lawn. The hostel was modern and very clean, and with a capacity for two hundred tourists. There was a fine view over the Trondheim fjord, the Munkholmen fortress, and the nearby mountains. How quickly the time went, and how happy I was to work in such ideal surroundings. While working in the garden one morning a blonde girl suddenly ran towards me, she had remembered me working in the garden of the Oslo youth hostel two years before. Her Brother spent much time in work concerning the migration of birds in various European lands, and she had also joined him in Poland, Germany, and Sweden. She was now working as a guide at a museum at Harlem in Holland. One evening we spent almost two hours watching a heavenly sunset from the hostel lounge. The sky, mountains, and quiet waters of the fjord slowly changed from one shade of colour to another as the glow of the bright sunset changed into a darkening twilight . The warden and his wife were extremely friendly, and lost no time in taking me out in their car and showing me something of the older parts of the town and its wonderful surroundings. We went walking in the forests with their two sons, Peter and Gunnar, who took great delight in being at their element amongst the nature. As I walked with them at a brisk pace, breathing in the crisp air of the forested mountain slopes, I felt on top of the World.!! This was living in its true and finer sense, enjoying radiant health and being in perfect harmony with one's surroundings.!!

I recollected part of the Norwegian National Anthem "And, when night in falling, brings as dreams to Earth". So those carefree, happy days in the delightful old city came to an end. Indeed I felt rather sad as I walked slowly along the streets to the railway station. Crossing over the ancient bridge, chiefly constructed of wood, I paused to gaze over the winding River Nidda. The waters shone with a delicate brightness in the early rays of the morning sun, swallows flew silently overhead, and my senses were awakened with something so simple yet so great "Joy in Living".

Both on the lengthy journey and during my stay in Trondheim I had experienced so much, and still there was much more in store.

It seemed almost like England as the train passed through the fertile landscape of Southern Trondelag, with large prosperous farms with crops of oats and barley ripening in the warm sun, with stacks of hay hanging neatly on horizontal wires supported by wooden posts. How I admire the sturdy, hard-working Norwegian farmer, these fine, honest workers are an example to all of us, if we live in big towns or are fortunate to work in more rural surroundings. Once past the station at Storen, a slow ascent was began up the Drivdal valley which was narrow and thickly forested, giving away to a series of deep, winding ravines with the river Driva racing down steep slopes and cascading down high waterfalls.

At Oppdal the train made a welcome halt, so I took a short walk along the station, which had a splendid setting, amongst green meadows flanked by forested hills and mountains high. From here one can take regular buses to the port of Kristiansund and the fjords of the far-flung west-coast. Nearby was the high Sisselho mountain, renowned for its beauty and breathtaking grandeur. Every single minute I gazed at these splendid chain of mountains which I found both inspiring and almost magical in their everchanging splendour. I could have spent days just wandering over those wild slopes to appreciate their beauty even more. I noticed one or two old farm houses and barns with grass growing from the thick layer of turf on their rooves, with their structure of wood they blended so finely with their unspoilt surroundings.

As the altitude became higher, the forests were left far behind, and gave way to the rugged expanse of the Dovre mountains with their rocky outcrops and sparse vegetation of grasses, mosses and heather. To the right was the 7 thousand foot high Snohetta mountain, with its higher slopes glistening with eternal snow.!! The atmosphere was very clear, so I could see a great distance. A small group of Lapps was encamped by the road which followed closely the course of the swiftly flowing river, with their bright clothing, they could be distinctly seen. What a hard life they lead, in this region of long winters and very short summers, but living near nature must give them a sense of fulfilment.!! At Hjerkinn the track reached its highest point, well over 3 thousand feet. This area is rich in wild life, including a large herd of musk oxen. This herd was imported from Spitsbergen, and is thriving in its new domain. Soon we passed the Fokstu marshes, with their bird sanctuary. Norway is doing much by increasing her areas used as nature reserves, for until recently the wild-life has been sadly neglected. As an active member of the Norwegian Nature Conservation Society, I hope and sincerely believe that many others will do much to aid and encourage love and respect of wildlife.

On reaching Dombas, another halt was made at this small but important route centre. From here it is about 70 miles to the peaceful town of Andalsnes with the high mountains of the Sunnmore and Nordmore. I would have liked to have visited my friends Lars and Anne Marie, who ran a large youth hostel with energy and ability, but time was short. It became suddenly hot as the train left the Rondane mountains and entered the upper reaches of the Gulbrandsdalen valley. The swiftly flowing waters of the river Lagen were deep green, fed by glacial waters of the Rondane and Jotunheimen peaks. The Jotunheimen is the highest range in Norway, and the Glittertind and Galhopiggen are well over 8 thousand feet. On the small station of Otta was an ice-cream stall, and many of the passengers, perspiring freely, rushed for ice-cream and cool drinks.

The Gudbrandsdalen is the longest valley in the whole of Norway, and the river Lagen runs through its entire length. As the journey continued, I felt happy and relaxed as several villages and well built farmsteads were passed. Several of these farms have been owned by the same families and their descendants for many generations, some can even be traced back to the old chieftain families of the earlier days of Norwegian history. The farms were confined to the lower slopes, above were extensive forests of fine pines with beautiful deep golden red trunks, and even higher, meadows and rough pasture for summer grazing, known as saeters. The large wooden buildings and rustic fences were so picturesque in their warmth of colouring and simple beauty, and reminded me so much of some of the paintings I had seen at the National Gallery in Oslo.

At Lillehammar I managed to have a large cup of tea with lemon, so refreshing in a temperature well over eighty degrees fahrenheit. I have been to Lillehammar several times and the climate is dry and invigorating. Situated at the head of Lake Mjosa, with a population of 12,000, it has both cultural and historical connections. Sigrid Undsted, a famous writer lived here, and on a steep mountainside, is the Maihaugen open-air museum, the largest in Norway. Twelve miles away, at Aulestad, is the home of Bjornstjerne Bjornson, of world-wide literary fame. The Art Museum contains modern and 19th paintings by Edvard Munch, Christian Krogh, and those of J. C. Dahl. The National Gallery also contains some of Dahl's masterpieces, and I find their love of Norway's splendid landscape an ever-increasing delight.!!

On the mountains are the resorts of Sjosjoen and Nordseter which, during the months from Christmas to Easter, are a paradise for Skiing, sunshine, and scenery. The paddle-steamer "Skibnader" is the only one of its kind still used in Norway, ever since 1856 it has sailed the whole length of Lake Mjosa, from Lillehammar to Minnesundet.

South of Lillehammar the softer scenery and lower hills covered with prolific vegetation had an almost southern atmosphere almost like that of Devon or Somerset. Just south of the lake, at Eidsvoll, the first Norwegian Constitution of 1814 was founded. By late evening the express-train arrived at Oslo East Station, and a total distance of three thousand miles had been traversed ,well into the Arctic regions of Scandinavia. How fortunate I was to have experienced so much and gained knowledge of the people and customs of the wild Arctic region which still fortunately retains something of the old pioneer spirit.!!

How delighted I was to meet some of my old friends and the staff at Haraldsheim, Oslo was still sweltering under an almost tropical heat wave. And the letters from home and elsewhere were a sheer delight in themselves. Work awaited me at the youth hostel, so I immediately commenced the following day, it was just like being at home, working in such beautiful and familiar surroundings. One Sunday, as I looked around the Town Hall, an Englishman who was a courier on a bus, asked me for two or three hours help as a guide around Oslo. I was only too pleased to assist them, and so was soon telling them something about the old Viking ships and the "Fram". Fridjof Nansen sailed in this ship on his Arctic expedition, where it lay icebound for three Winters, 1893–6. Later it was utilised by Otto Sverdrup to explore the land to the North of the American continent. Roald Amundsen sailed in this same ship to the Antarctic, 1910-12, and was the first to reach the South Pole.

The friendly group of tourists saw the Kon Tiki raft which sailed entirely at the mercy of wind and current for 5,000 miles across the Pacific from Peru in 1947. Tor Heyerdahl, four other Norwegians and a Swede made this courageous journey with the hope of proving that the Polynesians could probably have sailed to the Pacific Islands from South America, and not Asia, as had more often been assumed. I also took them around the Frogner Park, how delightful it was to simply take one's time admiring the splendour of the well stocked flower beds, especially the fine display of roses, as the climate here is not so suitable for rose and flower growing as in Denmark, which has a much milder climate.

The Frogner Park is renown for the Vigeland sculptures which are here in almost unbelievable numbers. An obelsk, fifty-five feet high, forms the apex of the sculpture park. From a personal point of view, I find the Greek sculptures of unusual inspiration, as they portray the feeling of radiant health of humans with their slim but strong and agile muscular bodies. The city gave Vigeland complete freedom to work and spend as

OSLO – with the Karl Johan, Parliament and Palace.

STOCKHOLM. The Royal Palace and Gamla Stad, the "Old Town".

he thought prudent, provided he devoted his work to the municipality. He signed the contract in 1921 and worked with all his energy until his death in 1943. I showed them something of the attractive shopping centre in Karl Johans Gate, and the Akershus Castle, which dates back to the 13th century.

How I remember and treasure those happy, carefree days, both working at "Haraldsheim" and assisting a few families with their gardens. It was fun helping the active hard-working Mr. Lie, and his homely American wife, he always had a strong sense of humour and an extremely alert mentality. Mr. Karvang, the dentist had a garden with a heavenly view over the Oslo Fjord, he was very musical with an almost southern temperament, he also played me some gipsy music as I helped him on a gloriously warm August day, as sailing ships glided effortlessly across the sparkling waters below.!! September came, to me a month of inner peace and strength, with the air becoming fresh and invigorating, and the trees taking on their initial Autumn tints. Gone were the thousands of tourists from the city, and even in the heart of Oslo, it was just as if Nature was taking a well-earned rest.

Several times I visited the National Art Gallery and each time I gained an ever-growing joy amongst the delicate beauty of the utterly dedicated painters. And what masterpieces many of these men have produced. Time will pass, but their beauty will remain and increase in intensity. A sincere respect for Nature influenced the works of J. C. Dahl in the early nineteenth century. Here too one can view the works of Thomas Fearnley, such as Labrofossen, depicting a mountain river in full spate, with high fells partly covered by cloud and mist. Thomas Fearnley was perhaps the most important pupil of Dahl, he certainly possessed the same romantic idealism. My favourite painting is "The Hardanger Wedding" by Adolph Tidemand and Hans Gude.

This is a masterpiece, with the bride and bridegroom in national costume, surrounded by other members of their family as they make their journey to their new home on the farm. In the distance is the homely wooden church, with friends waving, as if to convey their love and deeply moving good-will.!! The calm waters of the fjord mirror the rocky shores, the slender silver birches which grow right to the water's edge, while a high waterfall pours down from a sheer precipice on the opposite shore. Still higher the mountains rise to peaks covered by snow, glistening brightly in the sunshine, under a sky so blue.!!

Gerhard Munthe, Christian Krogh. and Harriet Becker were able, by sheer devotion and steady patience at their work, to represent typical Norwegian people, customs, nature and romantic landscape.!! Edvard Munch was also a greatly talented artist, some of his works are in the National Gallery, while most of his important pieces are housed in the Monch Museum. These Norwegian painters loved their land and its never-ending charm. They knew all too well the intense struggle which the nature presented to its sturdy, inventive inhabitants. Their paintings brought them even nearer to the splendour of the Norwegian characteristics, from the peasant on the farm, the graceful birch by the stream, to the eternal snow of the mountain peaks.!!

Hans Heyderdahl was a remarkable artist, for he portrayed the life of the ordinary people so much, especially the facial expressions and simple yet warm and congenial ways of the fishermen and hard-working farming folk. And although many of the country inhabitants were poor, they often lived a very rewarding life, as they lived in close contact with an environment of unusual beauty and charm.

August Cappelen had works of such great talent that they are still in pride of place in the National Gallery. His life was sadly very short, and he only lived until the age of 25. Ever since a boy he had a great love and appreciation of the nature which he lived amongst in Telemark. Like me, he found lasting delight in the forest, hills, rivers, and mountains of Telemark, and this made a lasting impression and brought out his kind and gentle nature.

So September portrayed two sorts of splendid paintings, the dedicated patience of Norwegian painters, and the brilliant colours and hues of the parks and gardens of Oslo.

Just before I left Oslo, in early October, I went to the National Theatre, and enjoyed every moment of a lively, humorous comedy by Ludvig Holberg. The theatre was founded in 1726, and has something of atmosphere and culture which gives me simple joy and dignity each time I see it, in sunshine or in rain. Once or twice, on a Sunday, I sensed the joy of freedom as I went out walking in the forests which mean so much for the citizens of the capital.

The leaves fell slowly off the trees, forming a soft, rich gold and brown carpet on the ground below. The night sky became ever clearer, bright and radiant with a multitude of stars, which had a wondrous fascination in their infinite beauty. Ice formed on the ponds, frosts turned the roofs and lawns into a sparkling white as each new day dawned.!! Reluctantly, filled with gratitude and sentiment, I bade farewell to that far-flung, attractive city I had grown to love so much.

I left by the early morning train to Bergen, every minute the journey was a sheer joy, for I was able to experience the everchanging colours of Autumn as I journeyed west. Large pockets of hoar frost covered the lower valley slopes, giving the surroundings an enchanted appearance, higher up in the mountains the forest was a rhapsody of colour. The quiet beauty of the idyllic landscape made the journey almost a blessing divine, and a truly fitting ending to this long, eventful Summer living and working in Norway the Sublime.!!

KARLSTAD – The Jewel of Sunny Varmland.

BERGEN: the 800 year old Fantoft Stave Church was destroyed by fire in 1992 but is to be rebuilt.

How I rejoiced when I returned to Norway the following Spring. It was early May, and on the train journey from Bergen to Oslo, I decided at stop at Al in Hallingdal. My friends, Ivar and Esther, the teachers, lived here, and we were all delighted to meet after the passage of two years. By the time I reached their home, it was late evening, and although it was Spring, the night was very chilly. The following morning I took a long walk up into the mountains, here the snow was often knee deep, but the warmth of the sun was already making it melt rapidly. It was wonderful seeing the first green buds on the trees, and the initial traces of animal, bird, and insect life. I quite enjoyed that day of restful relaxation before leaving by the evening train to Oslo.

In the east of Norway, it seemed so strange, seeing high drifts of snow near the railway, and small lakes still covered with ice. Only three days before I had been working in Torquay amongst gardens with a multitude of flowers and shrubs in full bloom under a warm, sunny sky. And yet my heart thrilled to the eternal call of the North, the wide open spaces, the mountains forests, and lakes, and the swift transition from Winter into Spring, and Summer.!! The dusk slowly descended over the lonely mountains and deep, forested valleys, and by the time I arrived at the Oslo East Station it was already dark. As I alighted from the train, it was so good to see the familiar streets and landmarks, as I caught the tram to the suburbs. As I walked with my heavy rucksack from the terminus, I instantly noticed the Haraldsheim youth hostel brightly illuminated against a background of high hills under a bright, starry sky. This was my true "Home from home", where I lived and worked, and met many people from all over the world. A warm glow of contented happiness crept into my mind as I climbed the long, steep slope to the hostel.

And in just a few brief days Winter had changed into Spring, and the growth was fast and luxuriant, especially the fruit trees which were soon a mass of brightly coloured blossom. The first person I helped was Mrs. Wagner, she, as her name signifies, was also highly musical, and had a delightful garden on the outskirts of Oslo. Another family I had the good fortune to help were Mr. and Mrs. Bay. Mr. Bay, in his eighties, was very active and alert, going to his office early every day. I helped Sven and his happy, friendly wife, Birgit, Sven spoke fluent English, he had never been in England, and yet had a fine collection of English books. I bought a second-hand cycle from Sven and found it quite useful for small trips, the nature in the close proximity of Oslo was still unspoilt in numerous places.

I decided to visit Stockholm, and caught the night express from Oslo. As I had worked in this "Venice of the North" in 1952, it would be highly interesting to see how much progress and change had been made since I was there. As the train passed through East Norway it followed the course of the River Glomma for a great distance. It was quite dark, with a cloudy sky, sometimes an isolated shaft of light was reflected on the smoothly flowing waters of the wide river, the longest in Norway.

Sleep overcame me, and when I awoke I found, that I was already in Sweden. The tall pine and fir trees stood outlined like silent sentinels against the clear, cold night sky with stars twinkling bright and strong.!! The region was sparsely inhabited for this is the West of the province of Varmland, of immense variety, beauty, and charm, with industrious, hospitable people.

Slowly the stars vanished from the sky as the first signs of dawn were shown on the eastern skies. As the light became more distinct, I took delight at seeing the solitude of the lakes and forests, there was an abundance of bird and wild-life on the streams and lakes. Through the dead traces of the previous year's growth were the fresh green shoots of the early Spring grass and low shrubs while the willow and birch trees were mirrowed in the quiet waters.

At Karlstad, the provincial capital of this large wooded land, the train made a lengthy halt. Karlstad has a very picturesque setting, on the shores of Sweden's largest lake, Lake Vanern, and also at the mouth of the Klara Alv river, where millions of logs are floated down each year to the sawmills. And true garden lovers cannot fail to visit the Rottneros mansion further to the north, with its carefully preserved sculptures and large ornamental gardens. The great Swedish writer, Selma Lagerlof, lived at Marbacka and found constant inspiration from the forests, wide skies, and the Lake Fryken which came right to the lower slopes of the mansion grounds. This is a truly splendid province, of sky and water, forests and hills, for everywhere one goes, one is surrounded by the fascinating variety of beautiful, unspoilt nature.

The town was still engulfed in its timeless peaceful charm as the train resumed its journey eastwards, with the sun shining brightly on the sleeping homes and buildings. It made me recollect a poem I had written.

R.P.

Selma Lagerlof whose writings have given joy throughout the world.

CHAPTER 6

VARMLAND — SWEDEN.

Clouds float like ships across the skies so blue
Birches green sway gently in the breeze
Here are woods and valleys
Far from the city's noise and hue
Where one finds peace and joy
And friends so kind and true!!

Still further eastwards the train sped, amidst almost continuous forests of fine pines, spruces, and birches, giving way to large farmsteads on low plainlands, with here and there a wooded hill in the distance. There was so much space, I almost imagined it to be in Poland or the Soviet Union, where I have also been by train. The fields amongst the woods were already a carpet of fresh green, with the rapidly growing shoots of Autumn sown oats, wheat, and barley. Passing over a few bridges amongst the lakes to the west of Stockholm, the suburbs with their high blocks of flats and bustling factories were passed with amazing speed, and the train pulled into Stockholms central station. Nowhere have I seen such a modern and well-planned station, not only was it almost ahead of the times, it was also beautiful and bright in its sweeping architecture and practical design. In the station hall were several kiosks and shops selling everything from a postcard to a shirt, and also two or three excellent snack-bars and first-class restaurant.

As I left the station, I was amazed how the city had changed since I worked there. Everywhere many of the older buildings had been demolished, to make room for wider streets and office flats. Considering the size of Stockholm, I thought how smoothly the traffic flowed in the very heart of this fine city.

The cold morning air aroused my appetite, and the fresh aroma of hot coffee from a cafe attracted my attention. Finding a small restaurant at Tegelbacken, I sat by a window, and was well rewarded with a splendid view of the Royal Palace, the busy Vasa bridge, and the waters of Lake Malar, reflecting the bright sunshine on its deep blue surface. For a few moments I forgot the noisy traffic and bustle of the streets, and I was in a world of my own.!!

As I resumed my walk, I noticed a nearby fisherman who was engaged catching a few fish in his wide nets, only a few yards from the Royal Palace. I passed the Royal Opera House, which is one of the oldest in Europe. It is not far from the Stadsholmen island, the centre of the old Stockholm town, which today is extremely well preserved as a historical monument of lasting greatness. A mere 5,000 people live here, a further 15,000 travel from the suburbs each day to work here.

And so I continued my stroll into downtown area of Stockholm, this is just North of Strommen, this is a stretch of water around which the older buildings, harbour, and ramparts of the town were built. Strangely enough, although three quarters of the Stockholmers live in the suburbs, two thirds work in the central parts of the city.

Sweden was fortunate enough to look ahead with the problem of traffic in the larger towns. As far back as 1940, when the town only had a population of 800,000, the interest was strong and the initial steps to build the subways was taken. By 1945, work was in full progress, and by 1957, the first system of subways had 47 stations and 25 miles of track. This network connects the western and southern suburbs to the city centre. In addition, a second subway system joins the south western suburbs with the centre, and is being expanded to reach the north-eastern areas. And vast sums are being wisely invested to improve the road communications within the city. The Stockholmers had the common-sense to be drastic enough to widen many of the streets and closed some to enable the citizens to enjoy shopping on foot.

At Hotorgs city, the old houses have vanished, and now a splendid shopping street to be used only by pedestrians has taken shape. What is perhaps no less important, the Stockholmers look forward forgetting their fascinating past. Much effort has been exercised to preserve the historical buildings and preserve many of the beautiful views of this progressive town.!!

As I walked along the Wide Strandvagen, it was refreshing watching the brightly glittering waters of the Nybroviken, while numerous office blocks and artistic shops flanked the tree-lined avenue. This rather long and immensely interesting walk came to a pleasant end as I entered the buildings of the Swedish Radio.

The first person who approached me was Mr. Jan Nystrom, the programme director of the English-American section. As he had lived in England, and was very attached to the Westcountry and Dartmoor, we had much to discuss. At lunch I was joined by Victor, a friendly enterprising Londoner, and Trevor, from New Zealand. They made a recorded interview about my work and travels, as they were very keen to learn more about an Englishman's outlook and experiences. After leaving the Swedish Radio House I found time to visit the Old English Church, it was just as if part of England had taken root on a foreign soil, giving an undescribable pleasing atmosphere to its immediate surroundings. It was like being on home ground again.!!

Before catching the train to Norway, I spent some of the evening exploring the town centre. I took a long stroll by the waterfront, and found the perfect blending of land, water, and sky to be an eternal source of beauty and charm which gives Stockholm a special fascination of its own. The beauty is not only fascinating, it is also inspiring. Looking across the wide stretch of Lake Malar, the numerous lights were reflected on its darkening waters.

Finishing a light supper at the central station, I felt just content watching people of all types crowd through the station and after boarding the express train, the warmth of the compartment made my tired muscles gently relax before going off into a blissful sleep.!!

And when I awoke, the low early morning sun was shining on the lonely forests and lakes of Varmland, not far from the Swedish frontierl As I gazed on the sleeping farmsteads and high forested hills with stil· traces of the winter's snow, that bustling, great city seemed so remote like a past dream, more romantic than real.!!

In Eastern Norway, clouds slowly enveloped the sweeping hills and a steady drizzle set in. At the small town of Kongsvinger, noted for its timber and paper mills, early workers alighted most of them seemed rather tired and still not fully awake. I have experienced exactly the same with passengers in London, Warsaw, Rotterdam, and elsewhere. It made me realise how much mankind all over the World has in common, as they set out for their daily work.

As for me, I prefer to meet other fellow-mortals during a relaxing evening, or at the week-end. For then we can talk and join in mutual understanding in a truly festive spirit. This is the deep human warmth of brotherhood which we should, and generally can, share with others.

These thoughts remained in my mind for a considerable time, and acted as a mental stimulus to be more positive and optimistic in my everyday life.!! When I arrived in Oslo I felt tired and stiff after the long journey and yet I felt determined to make a brief visit to the Norwegian Radio and perhaps have some good fortune. Going by tram or bus would have taken a considerable time, so I went by taxi to save time and energy. Luck came my way, and after endless searchings and meetings, a smiling Norwegian made a recorded interview for a topical morning programme. Then it was back to work again.

How difficult the day seemed as the tiredness of the journey still remained as I worked in the garden. This made me more than ever realise what a trying life many of the actors, doctors, and politicians must have had. Their hectic lives were in no way to be envied. Far happier to be humble and sincere.!!

As May came to an end, I made the trip to Andalsnes by train. It is a highly enjoyable experience to travel the seventy miles from Dombas, high up in the Dovre mountains, to the plain of the Isfjord, where the unspoilt small town of Andalsnes welcomes the traveller from afar.!! The Rauma line was opened in 1924, and opened an area of outstanding beauty in a very remote and little known region.

As the train left Dombas, it passed through coniferous forests which cover the lower slopes of Mount Dovre. The jura bridge, was crossed, and below the Jura river cascaded through a deep, rocky strown ravine. At Lesja, a small mountain community, a short stop was made, and to the south were magnificent vistas of the Kjolen mountains, vast and uninhabited. Further west these mountains were followed by Mount Tverrfjell, which has much steeper slopes, almost forming a sudden transition from the east to the western Norwegian landscape. Here, near the single track, was Lake Lesjaskogsvatn, this smiling lake forms a watershed, and from its waters rivers flow both towards the east and west. All the way from Lillehammar I had followed the course of the River Lagan, and now I was closely following the track of the River Rauma, which empties into the sea.

As Bjorli was reached, the railway line zig-zagged through the woods and on either side high wooden fences had been constructed as a protection against the high falls of snow. St. Olav is said to have passed this way on his long trek in 1028, from Valdal to the Gudbrandsdalen when he was forced to flee from Norway. Bjori marks the point where the peaceful scenery of East Norway suddenly gives way to the impressive and inspiring grandeur of the West.!! To the west rose the snow-capped peaks of the Romsdal alps, with peaks up to 6,000 feet, such as the Venjetind. And so the Oppland county was left, and before me was the splendour of the More county and the wild Romsdal valley.!! Borja is the mountain which marks the entrace to the Romsdal valley, and is very close to the railway, on the western side. How I thrilled at the spectacle of the cascades of streams and waterfalls which often drop vertically for many hundred feet, fed by the eternal snows of the higher slopes. The Rauma river races on, tumbling over steep precipices and amongst boulder strown ravines. Then came a rapid descent, passing the one mile long Stavem tunnel, which makes a complete turn inside the mountain. When the train emerged from the tunnel, it continued in the opposite direction, immediately below the line above. I had a wondrous view of the Verma falls, which plunge vertically 1,250 feet from the cliff top. Again the train slowly entered the mountain, into the Kylling reverse tunnel which makes a massive gradual curve within the mountain and as the train left the long tunnel, it passed over the Kylling bridge, and I saw the river Rauma 200 feet below, foaming and thundering through a narrow gorge.

I looked up, and saw the railway line at two levels above me, it had traversed five miles in this double curve to bring it a mere 330 feet lower

STOCKHOLM – The Venice of the North.

Olavinlinna Castle near SAVONLINNA in Karelia.

down in the valley. The valley slowly widened and became more level, and the river flowed at a more gentle pace. The mountain sides were so steep that I had to crane my neck to catch a glimpse of some of the summits. From a dizzy height waterfalls hurtled down the mountain side like shining silver bands and I gazed at the famous "Bridal Veil", of splendid, untamed grandeur. The valley was green, fertile, and well cultivated, for centuries the farming population have lived and worked in this valley, working long hours during the short Summer, and during the dark Winter months they were busy with carpentry, tapestry, and other work which could be done in the home.

To my left soared the Trolltindene peaks, so steep that no snow will lie on their slopes which are devoid of vegetation. Here is the highest vertical rock face in Europe, Trollveggen, the precipice is over 3,000 feet in height, and reaches out towards the top of Trollryggen, over 6,000 feet high. And to my right the mighty Romsdalhorn appeared.

And so the train finally arrived in Andalsnes station, which had surroundings just as fascinating as the journey from Dombas. It had a small, tidy flower garden, and tall chestnut trees which looked so dignified, green, and fresh in the bright sunshine. I walked along the quiet streets and small patches of meadowland which encroached right to the very centre of this community with unique qualities. Avenues of slender birches swayed gently in the sea-breeze, apple and cherry trees were in full blossom, and the cottages were painted in a most colourful manner.!!

Making my way towards the southern edge of the town, I sat down on a hillside for about two hours, deeply moved by the splendid panorama of sea, islands, mountains and valleys. Everywhere I turned I was surrounded by beauty.!!

I could have gazed even longer at this heavenly view, but by now I was beginning to experience the needs of a healthy appetite, and so at the nearest hotel I ordered an evening meal. As I ate my supper, it was remarkable to be able to look out of the nearby window, and watch the evening sun shining over the blue waters of a fjord, and high, snow capped mountains which were too numerous to count. It was only a simple meal, but the setting was fit for a king.!! The low sun sank below the mountains, majestic in their silent grandeur, and I retraced my steps to the station, where the night-train for Oslo was waiting to depart.

As the train slowly gathered speed, I had a strong feeling of sadness and nostalgia to leave this splendid setting. It was such a pity to leave behind the beauty which had moved my very heart and soul.!! A bright, full moon lit up the darkening twilight, it was like some enchanted dream.!! As the train approached the valley immediately below the Trolltindene peaks their huge outlines threw shadows across the sleeping farms and meadows. The train continued on its journey, climbing higher and higher amongst the rushing mountain streams, dark pine forests, and steep mountain slopes, which could be quite distinctly seen in the bright moonlight. It was already midnight, and so a new day dawned on this region of high mountains and isolated valleys which had inspired poets, painters, and idealists so strongly. How grateful I felt to have been able to visit the Romsdal and the fjord town of Andalsnes, and depart with lasting admiration and attraction for the fascinating splendour of their wonderful surroundings.

THE SPIRES OF UPPSALA CATHEDRAL RISE ABOVE THE HISTORIC UNIVERSITY CITY.

The joy of Springtime in Balestrand.

An old Norwegian stabbur on a farm at Dagali, near the road from Geilo to the Numedal

R.P.

CHAPTER 7

A WELCOME RETURN TO MY BELOVED TRONDHEIM

One warm evening in early June, as I had just finished a day's work, I received a long distance telephone call from Trondheim. The hostel warden, Rolf, informed me that he desperately required my help with the garden,. This came as a complete surprise, as I had already planned taking on some work in Sweden at the thriving port of Gothenburg. And I also changed my route, at the very last moment. Instead going directly by express train to Trondheim, I decided to first travel to Stockholm, and from there travel through central and northern Sweden, and cross over the mountains into Norway.

Leaving Stockholm late in the evening, the train did not take long to leave the high buildings and modern suburbs behind, and crossed the fertile farmlands of Uppland. Uppland is the ancient historical and cultural centre of Sweden, and from here the Viking fleets sailed great distances. They penetrated far down the entire length of the river Volga, and these courageous explorers founded the ancient Russia. There was a close connection between Swedish Uppland and the Anglo-Saxon kingdom of East Anglia, where the settlers practised the cults of the heathern gods before the advent of Christianity.

At the Cathedral town of Uppsala the train made a lengthy halt. Uppsala has a splendid botanical garden and a university of a very high reputation and standard, and it was here where the Sveas made pagan sacrifices to their gods, Oden, Fro, and Tor. It was twilight as the train left Uppsala, and it seemed just as if civilisation had been left behind in the passing of just a few minutes.!! The large, prosperous farms became less numerous, and forests of coniferous trees grew high above the railway track, which ran as straight as an arrow through the almost level plainland. By midnight I was fast asleep, and did not awake until the early hours of the morning. The morning sun was low on the horizon, and on all sides were high, rolling hills covered with thick forests as far as the eye could see. Sometimes I saw an isolated farm which had been built in a forest clearing. The hay had been hung up, suspended on wires between wooden posts, to dry, while the sloping meadows were a light green with masses of bright yellow buttercups mingling with the rapidly growing grass. How wonderful for such huge forests to grow so far north, where snow remains on the ground for six months of the year.!!

Later in the morning the train reached Sundsvall, a veritable oasis in this northern wilderness. Sundsvall is the most important town and the largest port in Northern Sweden, with its wide, tree lined avenues, parks, modern buildings and splendid town-hall. From here timber, wood pulp and other valuable forest products are exported in enormous quantities, apart from the months when the port is ice-bound. From Sundsvall the train headed in a more westerly direction, and the landscape was even more spectacular. For much of the time the railway line followed closely the winding River Ljusnan, which was often extremely wide and flowed at a slow pace through the lonely forests.

At Ostersund, a large cummunity situtated on Lake Froson, I was able to eat a quick breakfast on the station. One of my first geography lessons given by a delightful mixture of most polite and helpful Swedes was the undisputed fact that Ostersund was considered the exact centre of Sweden. And yet it was as far from the extreme south of Sweden as Inverness was from Penzance.

From the mountains above the straggling town, there is a splendid view across Lake Froson towards the mountains of Jamtland. The Swedish poet and writer Peterson Berger was able to find lasting inspiration and pleasure as his highly sensitive and creative writing clearly portrays.

Then came the most scenic and mountainous part of the journey to Trondheim. The line slowly climbed amongst the mountains, following closely the winding valley of the Indalsalven I could see ranges of high mountains towards the south and west, their peaks glistened with snow in the clear atmosphere. At Are, a popular skiing resort, several tourists alighted, with its nearby mountain huts and small guesthouses, it made an ideal holiday centre for those unfortunate beings who spent most of their lives in the big cities. The trees became shorter as a higher altitude was reached, and from Duven to the Norwegian frontier the terrain was often very swampy, with stunted pines and dwarf mountain birches growing on the slightly higher ground. After leaving Storlien I was once again in Norway.

The descent on the Norwegian side was very rapid, for the westward side of the mountain chain which forms a natural frontier between the two lands has a much steeper gradient. Splendid forests of high pine, fir, and spruce grew on the mountain sides, and following the river Stjorsdalselv, lower ground was reached. The temperature rose rapidly and I found the sudden heat quite oppressive. Passing the small village of Hell, with its appropriately named station, I burst into hearty laughter, the place is well known by tourists who make the journey often just to receive a single or return ticket. From the sea a cooling breeze made the heat more bearable, and many of the local inhabitants were basking in the sun, or taking a swim. My journey of over a thousand miles since leaving Oslo was coming to a close, and the thought of relaxing, worthwhile garden work already filled my tired mind.!!

At the hostel the warden, Rolf Kvam, and his industrious wife Inger made me so welcome, and in no time a splendid meal was set before me, by Rolf, who was an excellent cook. The two sons, Peter and Gunnar were highly interested in my travels and from time to time would join me and ask many a question about my work and travels. Rolf, Gunnar and I drove out to a market garden and selected about three hundred shrubs for the hostel garden. The land on which the youth hostel was built was very very rocky with masses of weeds and high grass everywhere, and plenty of shrubs would make the garden more beautiful and easy to maintain.

The nursery owner was a typical hard-working, honest Norwegian, tall and blond, he had deep blue eyes which radiated humour and good-will.!! He talked about his experiences when he worked in America, and we soon became firm friends. So, after getting rid of most of the weeds, I was soon occupied planting the shrubs, chiefly berberis and cotoneaster, which are very hardy and thrive in spite of poor soil conditions and hard frosts. A heat wave set in, something very unusual for this town only two hundred miles south of the Arctic Circle. The temperatures soared into the middle eighties, it was in fact several degrees warmer than places in Italy and Spain. But I quite enjoyed the heat, for I was able to drink plenty of lemonade and perspired freely.

In Trondheim is the oldest newspaper in Norway, the "Adressavisen" which is over two hundred years since its first publication. The newspaper offices are quite near the Cathedral and oldest part of the town, and it was refreshing to be given a long interview for an article in the following day's edition. A family who recognised me from the time when we met at the youth hostel in Gothenburg asked me to celebrate Midsummer Eve at their home. How I perspired in the humid heat and yet meeting Aslaug and Erling gave me much happiness, for it is indeed seldom to meet old freinds far away from home. About 11 p.m. I bade farewell, thanking them for an enjoyable evening, and as I walked slowly up the hill to the youth hostel, was rewarded by a splendid sunset. As the sun slowly sank below the mountains, the sky was a bright crimson which was transformed into a gentle purple glow which lasted intil midnight.

Another welcome surprise awaited me when I arrived at the hostel, and I was invited to join the warden, his wife, and brother-in-law on a midnight tour of Trondheim. I felt very tired, but was nevertheless delighted to join them. We saw the "Stiftsgarden, this is the largest wooden building in Northern Europe, and has been a royal residence since the crowning of Haakon VII in 1906. It is about two hundred years old and is both vigorous and elegant. Many of the old wooden houses were built with the combined efforts of local craftsmen and foreign artisans. After taking a long stroll in the wooded hills behind the town we drove down a long, tree lined avenue. It was named "Fridjof Nansensveien", a very fitting name in memory of a fine Scandinavian idealist.!! Returning to the town centre, we made a brief visit to the harbour, the ships were still on calm blue waters under a bright cloudless sky. And, passing the Old fortress of Kristiansen, we returned, happy and tired, to sleep through a night without darkness.!!

After work I would often sit on a park bench and watch the people and traffic pass by. The shopkeepers of Trondheim were both extremely charming and patient, and this made shopping, or merely shopgazing, a pleasure to cherish.!! I often spent an odd hour in my favourite bookshop near Var Frue Church, and how I wish, with all my heart and soul, that there were not more shops like it. For Trondheim had a delightfully peaceful and relaxed atmosphere and here time seemed meaningless. Here people knew how to really live.!!

Immediately after planting the shrubs I spent two days giving them a thorough watering to ensure they would survive the hot weather. Then I returned to Oslo for a short time to do some more essential work. On my return to Trondheim I was able to build a small wall and planted some more bushes. This time the weather was much cooler and often drizzle set in, which was not so pleasant. And I was able to have a recorded interview on the local radio. I enjoyed the talk very much, feeling both happy and completely relaxed, and made this visit to Trondheim have a sense of fulfilment.!! It made the extra effort and long wait well worthwhile. It was dull and overcast when I left this town of timeless charm, and I felt rather sad when I said goodbye to the warden and his wife, as it would be a long time before I again had the opportunity of revisiting Trondheim.

I worked for a short time in Gothenburg, and in some ways it was being almost at home again, as I knew the town very well and had grown very fond of it for sentimental reasons. And although it is the most industrialised city in Sweden, with the biggest shipbuilding industry in the whole of Scandinavia, it had many splendid parks and gardens even near the very centre of the town. Each day I left early in the morning to cycle to my work, it was so quiet and peaceful, I even saw an occasional deer and several hares in the woods surrounding the town. It was also a splendid form of healthy relaxation in good weather.

During the evening it was always a joyous occasion visiting friends I had known for several years. My Scotch friend John and his Swedish wife Anika made me so welcome, drinking tea with them always made me think of dear old England. A Swedish engineer Ragnar, his wife Karin and brother Tore were very kind and helpful. Ragnar, although in his late seventies, was very active working in his home and helping others too. He was a sincere and ardent worker for peace and fostering international goodwill, his son Kjell had adopted two foreign children into his happy home. The youth hostel was on the city outskirts, which was rather unfortunate, as I missed my favourite abode at Stora Katrinelund near the central station, now unfortunately closed. Still, the warden was good-humoured and sympathetic, and some of the tourists were simply wonderful, so optimistic and enthusiastic about their travels and holidays.

But I always tried to avoid Gothenburg in the late afternoon, the traffic in the town was beyond a joke, even the city buses and trams were held up in traffic jams, and in wet weather the odd spots of oil made some of the streets quite slippery. But the parks were superb, especially the "Tradgardsforeningen" near the station, and the Botanical gardens, further south. And the Slottsskogen park had large lawns and fine beech and oak trees. Here the winters are much milder than most parts of Sweden, and the summers are not so dry. How beautiful the evenings are in this busy port, especially when one views the harbour from the Gotaalv bridge, with many miles of ships, large and small, gaily illuminated, while in the background brightly lit blocks of flats merged into the high wooded hills and deep purple skies. The Swedes revel in those warm Summer evenings and at the Liseberg, the equivalent of the Tivoli in Copenhagen, they certainly knew how to enjoy themselves. Most of the towns and even the smaller villages have open-air pavilions for dancing and entertainment, the short but glorious summer means so much to them. The concert house and theatre have some fine productions, and the new library has an excellent selection of books in many languages. Fortunately Sweden not only produces engineers and scientists, but also doctors, teachers, and men of high ideals. The Nobel Peace prize, is always associated with Scandinavia, and also humanity, regardles of race, religion, or language.!!

Sweden also has an alcoholic problem, but fortunately it is confined to only a small proportion of the population. They generally accumulate near the railway station, cheap restaurants, and one or two streets near the town centre. In Oslo it is exactly the same, but for a foreign tourist it gives a false impression, making the unfortunate minority seem greater in numbers than they are in actual fact.

Sweden is one of the most peaceloving and progressive nations in the World, and with her policy of strict neutrality she acts as a wise and level-headed mediator between the power blocks. She does a terrific amount of trade between the western and communist lands, which in its turn promotes prosperity, tolerance, and international good-will.!! When I read about the suffering of innocent people in war-torn Vietnam, and the poverty of millions in many lands, I only wish that more could have the courage and initiative of the Swedes towards world-peace.

We do not need big cars, washing machines, or many other items of modern society, but poverty is a terrible, degrading thing which should never be tolerated. And affluence is often a sad companion, for one does not have to possess much to be happy, and when one owns less, one appreciates small things even more. There are many rich people who are poor, because they are sometimes mentally and spiritually poor, and often poor people are spiritually rich. Of course, this is only true in some cases, as wisdom is universal, One can find wisdom amongst all classes of mankind, from a university professor to the easy going countryman who finds great delight in the surroundings he grows to love and cherish.

CHAPTER 8

THE LONG JOURNEY TO FINNISH LAPLAND.

When my season's work in Norway had been finished, I left Oslo with the hope and intention of visiting Finnish Lapland, a journey of over a thousand miles. I left early in the morning, and on reaching Kil, near the town of Karlstad, in Varmland, I changed trains and headed towards Gavle, which saved time by not passing through Stockholm. Most of the district of Dalarna was thickly forested, and the towns were few and far between. The train also stopped at Sandvika, world-famous for its steel products, especially saws, which are of high quality and great durability.

By early evening I reached Gavle, a large impressive town with factories and harbour bustling with timber and cargo boats. One could also instinctly feel the influence of the long winters on the population, quite different to Denmark and Sweden's west coast. It was thrilling to find a comfortable seat on the express train which goes as far as Kiruna, in Swedish Lapland, and Narvik, the iron-ore port in Northern Norway. By the time the train arrived at Bollnas, an important road and rail centre, it was already night, and some of the people on the station wore thick overcoats. But in the train it was delightfully warm and relaxing, one might have been somewhere in southern Europe. It seemed rather difficult to realise I was in the north of Sweden amongst huge coniferous forests.

The compartment was rather overcrowded, but I managed to sleep most soundly for several hours, before waking to see the dawn breaking slowly over the silent hills. It was impossible to see very far as the forests were so thick, but when the train passed a newly cut clearing in the forest, or climbed up a high hillside, some splendid views were seen. During the night, several hundred miles of northern taiga had been traversed, and sometimes the towns were often over a hundred miles apart. What progress science had made, even in the wilderness of the endless forests.!!

And so Boden came into sight as the long train came round a gradual bend, slowly losing momentum. In Boden, Autumn was already in the crisp atmosphere, as I walked along the rather quiet streets before finding a snack-bar for a pot of tea and cakes. But I missed Norway, the town was beautiful and the gardens spacious and planned with insight. Yet there were no forested hills with gaily painted cottages as in a typical Norwegian town, the town was too modern to possess the atmosphere typical of less progressive places. Later in the day I made a bus trip to the port of Lulea, where some friends, Dan and Madelaine and their two small children lived.

Dan was eager to show me more of the town and its immediate surroundings, for which I felt extremely grateful. We drove to the western

A May morning in lower Flamsdalen, with Flam Church dating from 1667

Danish Tourist Office

HANS CHRISTIAN ANDERSEN'S HOUSE AT ODENSE ON THE MAIN LINE FROM ESBJERG TO COPENHAGEN. THE INTERESTING DANISH RAILWAY MUSEUM IS NEAR THE ODENSE STATION.

perimeter of the town, and climbed to the top of a high hill which was being turned into a ski-jump. The sun was slowly setting in the amber sky, and before me were dark green forests stretching to the hills on the horizon.

We then visited the ancient wooden church with its collection of church cottages huddling closely together. There were several hundred of these cottages, still most carefully preserved.

In these neat rows of cottages the traveller from afar could sleep and eat, tether the horses, and attend an important service or meeting. I was indeed surprised to see such cultural links so far north, for the population of the Northern provinces of Sweden was, and still is, very sparse.

Lulea is next in importance after Narvik for the export of iron ore from the huge mining area of Kiruna. Unfortunately the Gulf of Bothnia freezes over for several months, so the port of Narvik is used throughout the Winter. The docks were very extensive, modern, and efficient.

Returning to their home, the aroma of a delightfully cooked meal filled my nostrils as Dan opened the door. Madelaine had cooked a simple yet delicious meal of fish, potatoes, vegetables, and hard bread. And what a divine way to finish a highly eventful day by a crackling log fire.!! And how well I slept that night.!!

Madelaine's parents, Bertil and Lotte, were good friends I had known for many years while working in Gothenburg, so, when I left in the morning I sent a greeting to her parents. Dan worked for a road haulage firm, the wages and conditions were very promising, but the winters were so long and monotonous he intended to later work in Southern Sweden. Thanking them, for their spontaneous hospitality, I left Lulea by train, and at Boden made another journey towards the Finnish frontier. The single line traversed lonely forests and a maze of rivers and swampland, the scattered villages had typical Lapp names as the Lapp influence was strong. I was happy to reach Haparanda, and crossing the wide Tornetrask river, was once again in Tornio, on the Finnish side. The fertility of the soil was remarkable, and crops ripen extremely well in the very short Summer with almost perpetual daylight for about three months.

Kemi was the next stop, although only a town with a small population of about 35,000, it was a very important centre for the manufacture and export of wood products. As Finland's consumption of electricity doubles every ten years, she needs much hydro-electric power, and as the south is much flatter, most of the power comes from the rivers in the north. On the Kemi river new hydro-power plants have been constructed. Now began my most exciting and enjoyable part of the journey as I boarded the bus to Rovaniemi, the capital of Lapland and my final destination.

The road, which was paved for the initial few miles, followed closely the course of the Kemijoki river. Much of the immediate surroundings was well cultivated and the farms looked almost as neat as those in the south of Finland. Several farmers and lumbermen were in the rather packed bus which was rattling along at a high speed along the now unsurfaced dusty road. Both the narrow road and single track railway ran almost parallel and I noticed one or two power stations of an impressive size. As we sped north, the scenery was wilder and the farms were less numerous. Forests replaced the meadows of the smiling farmsteads, and towards the eastern horizon were high, gently sloping hills, known as Tunturi, they looked so weird in the swiftly descending twilight.

This wild, almost uninhabited landscape gave me a strange feeling of isolation and melancholy, which is not uncommon on a journey of great duration. Civilisation seemed so far distant, and only the noise of the engine was audible in the region of immense space and amazing silence. Would the bus ever arrive in Rovaniemi, I thought, as its headlights lit up the forest which grew right to the side of the winding road. Then, as the bus turned round a bend I caught my first glimpse of the distant lights of Rovaniemi, and as the oasis in the northern wilderness grew closer, their brightness was reflected in the smooth, swiftly flowing waters of the River Kemi.

How overjoyed I felt, for I knew this was the most northern town of this fascinating journey. The bus came to a sudden halt in the terminal, which was brightly lit in sharp contrast to the overcast dark sky which was thickly clouded with a foreboding of rain. The bus station was busy, vehicles arriving and departing, and the waiting room and restaurant was a mixture of loud music, local gossip, and a blending of cooking, the aroma of fresh coffee, and air thick with strong tobacco smoke.

I took a bus to the local youth hostel, and as the bus lumbered through the maze of newly constructed blocks of flats, office blocks, and administrative buildings, I had time to ponder . The town was certainly modern and progressive, but everywhere the atmosphere retained the old pioneer spirit, for it was still surrounded by virgin forests, vast expanses, and swift climatic changes.!! From the bus stop it was about ten minutes of walking to the hostel, the air was mild and damp, and when I stepped inside the door I found myself perspiring. The warden and his wife made me welcome, but I was so tired I felt too reluctant to hold a conversation of any length, so I politely said goodnight.

When I awoke the low sun was shining through a break in the fleeting clouds, and the pine and birch trees threw their long shadows over the moss covered stones and grassy slopes. It was quite surprising to meet two Englishmen as they are few in numbers compared with other continental tourists in Finland. They asked me to join them for breakfast, but I felt rather restless, and just had a cup of coffee and a sandwich. And as I waited for the local bus, a small boy appeared. In his hand was grasped a piece of paper, and he lost no time in handing it to me. On it was written a hurried question "My brother is a scout, are you a scout too? Unfortunately a bus came round the corner, so I waved goodbye to the cheerful boy with the unusually friendly dog. I felt so reluctant to leave him so suddenly.

As the bus slowly passed a school, I noticed the children playing in the courtyard, what a happy crowd they were. How good it would be to give them a lesson in English, I thought, it was an inner sense of duty which compelled me to get off at the next stop and walk at a brisk pace to the school gates.

After a short wait, a lady teacher, Miss Kuivalainen, introduced me to her class, and it gave me great pleasure to talk about my experiences and answer various questions. The teacher invited me to visit her husband, but time was short, so I headed for the bus terminal.

After writing a few hurried post-cards, I ate a hearty meal, it was so warm that it was difficult to keep awake. Outside a chilly wind blew, it was only the middle of September, but the bright Autumn colours on the neat avenues of trees made it seem like November.

The return journey was rather uneventful, but the rapid approach of Autumn contrasted to that in southern Sweden and the west coast of Norway. Even at noon the sun was low on the horizon, and the days had become much shorter. I changed trains at Kemi, Haparanda, and Boden. At Boden I boarded the express which was to take me 800 miles to Stockholm, and I made friends with an elderly lady who I had helped with her luggage.

As the train sped on and on, darkness fell over the endless forests and lonely hills, and I read a newspaper before falling asleep. And as daylight returned, the train was still amongst the forests, but here the trees were taller and more stately, for the growth period was several weeks longer. Some of the farms had extensive clearings for crops and pasture, and they looked quite prosperous. What courage and determination these farmers possess, to work extremely hard throughout the short Summer season before the first frosts returned. They have a lifelong struggle against the rigours of Nature.

South of Sundsvall, in the province of Halsingland, I saw the first apple tree, a sure sign that we were approaching a less extreme climate. And what giants some of the pine trees were, they must have grown and matured over a great passing of years, how I wished we had such forests in England.!!

The port of Gavle is the largest town in Sweden north of Stockholm, and the large buildings and factories were so completely different to the smaller towns I had seen further north. I could see the outlines of the masts of cargo and timber ships in the harbour, the streets were full of traffic on the move. The formerly half-empty train became almost completely full to seating capacity, as passengers and business men made their morning journey to Stockholm.

Once south of Galve the entire landscape changed slowly. North of Gavle, the long Winter and sparce population had resulted in most of the landscape still retaining its original wildness. But as the train moved towards Stockholm, larger areas of land were cultivated, and the population gradually increased. Near Boden the snow would remain for about six or seven months, here only three or four months. And here the timber grows three times as quickly as that in the Far North.

The weather in Stockholm was showery and dull, and the low clouds made the atmosphere heavy and oppressive. Still, there was much to do and much to see in this fine metropolis.!! The shopping centre caught my eye, if one had time one could spend days walking around in the various multistores. After buying a few presents and souvenirs for friends, I visited the Public Relations Department of the Swedish Railway, and thanked them for their help and advice. By the early evening the grey clouds had vanished, as if by magic, and the sky was bright with the warm glow of a splendid sunset.

Stockholm was revealed in all her fascinating beauty, time stood still, as if to let the onlooker receive and retain the splendour of this town of land, water, and wide skies.!!

I strolled through the busy streets, the majority of the Stockholmers were hurrying home, I just found it impossible to hurry, I just wanted to more fully appreciate the beauty of the sunset scene.!! As I reached the waterfront at Tegelbacken, not far from the Royal Palace, the tall and graceful outline of the town hall was silhouetted against the slowly darkening crimson glow of the western sky. I slowly retraced my steps and made my way towards the old sailing schooner "Af Chapman" which is now used as a youth hostel. Unfortunately, the hostel was already full to capacity, but I still retained a strong sense of inner peace and felt no disappointment as I walked down the gangway. And across the waters of Lake Malar a multitude of lights were reflected in unusual clarity in the mellow twilight.

While waiting for an old friend, Sture, who I had not seen for many years, I became engaged in conversation with a delightful Englishman, Mr. Martin, and an American, Jennifer Harris. They and other teachers were busy maintaining an Institute for personal Development and I found them highly interesting and alert.

They invited me to visit them at their college on the island of Vaxholm when I next visited Stockholm.

Sture drove me to his home in the suburbs and it was good to have some light refreshments with his family, and it was almost midnight before I returned to the small hotel where I had booked a room. I was quite saddened to catch an occasional glimpse of one or two solitary drug addicts as the underground train stopped at some of the stations. Unfortunately drug addicts are found in most of the big cities of the west, and I only hope that far more drastic measures will be taken to curb the drug smuggling.

Waking early in the morning, it was a pleasing sight to see the sun lighting up the nearby buildings, another fine day had dawned on this fair city. After a good wash and shave, I walked out into the streets, already busy with the morning traffic. I headed for the Af Chapman youth hostel, it would be pleasant to enjoy a breakfast on board this stationary ship, with a superb view over Lake Malar. The sun shone brightly on the calm waters of Strommen, how sleek and majestic the numerous bridges looked, darkly outlined against the glittering waters. After breakfast I returned to the city centre. While passing through a small park I was suddenly attracted towards a negro who was quietly sitting on a wooden bench. There was something about his kindly, calm face which attracted me, I was happy to know that he had studied at the same college as Martin Luther King.

And so it was farewell to Stockholm, as I looked out from the express train which was to take me to Gothenburg. How Gothenburg had changed. It was Summer when I was last there, with long, sunny days. But now Autumn was here, and the wind caught the falling leaves of the oaks, chestnuts, and beeches, sending them in a flurry across the wet pavements. There was no longer the gay atmosphere of a Summer town, the city dwellers, although smartly dressed and athletic in their posture, lacked their carefree, bright outlook of the Spring and Summer.

How quickly the time had passed, the short, splendid Spring, the warm, bright Summer days which mean so much to every Scandinavian, and now the mellow Autumn, which had come so slowly as to be at first completely unobserved. England beckoned, time had come to leave the Northern Lands.!!

It was farewell to the mountains, fjiords, forests, lakes, and rivers, of the Northen Lands. Happy memories of true and lasting friendships filled my heart and soul, and a feeling of strong sentiment and sincere gratitude were ever present. How fortunate I had been to have travelled so far and experienced so much.!!

A festive spirit reigned supreme as the Norwegian liner Venus sailed from Newcastle on May 17th., Norway's National Day. The evening was light and I felt so full of happy anticipation that sleep was almost impossible. Morning dawned bright and clear, and it was not long before the ship docked at Stavanger. It was three years since I last visited this lively town, and I lost no time in making the opportunity to visit the chief places of interest.

Luck came my way, and when I reached the offices of the Stavanger tourist manager, I was delighted to find him equally surprised to meet me. He offered to take me round the town on a sightseeing tour, and this invitation gratefully accepted. The early morning air was still crisp and invigorating, the kind of morning when the joy of living permeated one's very mind, body and soul. Happy and relaxed, Mr. Erling Herstad showed me some of the older parts of the town, and the humble, well painted cottages nestled closely on the steep rocky hillsides. These dwellings of true Norwegian dignity could tell many a tale of the seamen's struggles, sadness, and hopes. After storms and discomforts came the joy of a safe return to the haven amongst the fjords and windswept islands.

The older parts of the town also form the shopping centre, with winding streets, and thanks to careful preservation, are full of picturesque, old-world charm. The market place is situated between the harbour and the old cathedral, and with its vegetables, fruit, and flowers, is a perfect picture of colourful activity. Here stands the statute of Alexander Kielland the town's own poet. The Cathedral was designated by an English Bishop to an English saint St. Swithin. Stavanger is truly historic, founded as a trading centre by hard-working, enterprising local inhabitants. From this region Norway was made into one kingdom, and Sigurd Jorsalfar instigated the Bishopric.

Mr. Herstad showed me some of the modern suburbs, with their fascinating variety of bungalows and houses and tidy gardens. With its avenues of trees and splendid parks and gardens, and extensive farmland in the immediate surroundings, one could almost imagine oneself to be somewhere in Britain. Beech trees, oaks, and chestnuts grow and flourish equally as well as in the south of England, thanks to the warmth of the long Summer days and the mild influence of the Gulf Stream. And yet not so far away is the Lyse Fjord, with its famous "Pulpit" rock, two thousand feet above the deep blue waters, which makes one more fully appreciate the grandeur of the universe.

And Stavanger has a golf course with an almost English atmosphere, a place of relaxation for some of the town's 80,000 inhabitants. Stavanger can also boast of having a special college where one can learn everything on the fine art of canning fish. Students from many lands study here, even from Japan. Several million cans are distributed annually, mostly for export. But time was short, and waving my Norwegian host farewell, I saw his car disappear amongst the busy traffic of the city centre.

After a delightful cruise amongst the rocky coast and islands of the rugged west-coast, it did not take long before the port of Bergen was reached, it was rather windy and chilly and I got a thorough soaking from

GEIRANGER FJORD in all its splendour.

Spring returns to the Hardanger

a heavy shower while waiting patiently for a bus. But how joyous I felt as I walked up the steep road to the Montana Youth Hostel.!! Synnove, the warden's wife immediately made me welcome, and prepared some delioious sandwiches and tea "ad lib". The many lights of the town glittered in the valleys below, making the whole town take on the appearance of a fairyland.!! The birch trees swayed briskly in the strong wind, while wisps of cloud and mist covered the higher slopes of the nearby mountains.

After the hearty meal it was a sheer joy just to relax in the cosy lounge of the hostel, talk to some of the youthful tourists and watch the multitude of lights of Bergen's city, which seemed like endless strings of pearls threading along the valleys and terminating to the darkness of the hills.

After a sound sleep I awoke refreshed, and glancing from my window, I could see it looked like being a perfect day for travelling. At breakfast a French lady-teacher and a Japanese student joined me. The French lady was very much in love with Norway, the Japanese was more concerned with pop music and technical progress, I much preferred the outlook of the former, because in life, especially in the hectic rush of big cities, one needs far more imagination and sentiment.

Soon it was time to say a grateful farewell and catch a bus to the station. I always have a strange feeling of excitement and optimistic hope whenever I make a long train journey, and this was certainly no exception. For several miles the train ran parallel to the steep sides of Sorfjord, the high peaks were mirrowed in the still waters, waterfalls cascaded over the sheer rock faces, while in the distance I caught my first glimpse of snow, gleaming white under a brilliant blue sky. Spring had only just come, and only in the lower valleys were the trees showing their first green buds.

Here and there were small villages, and farmers preparing the rough ground for Spring sowing. Many of the farms were very small, with poor soil, and often horses were invaluable amongst the boulder strown terrain. Most of all I loved to see the smaller childern who waved to the passengers with boundless energy as if to say "Welcome to Norway". Many of the people rode on cycles, a handy means of transport from the farm to the nearest village.

Once past the tourist centre of Voss the terrain became more rugged. The fields slowly became replaced by splendid pine forests, and as the train slowly climbed up amongst the steep ravines, splendid vistas opened up from all directions. For me this is the most beautiful part of the Bergen Line, leaving the lush valleys of the western fjords, and climbing towards the high Hardanger Vidda, the mountains which later slowly descend to the eastern valleys.

The pine forests slowly merged with splendid birch trees and higher up the forest was predominantly of dwarf birches. What undescribable splendour, the snow still deep amongst the thickets, and the endless miles of mountain slopes both above and below. Little wonder that Ibsen, Holberg, and Grieg found spontaneous inspiration. The stunted birches became scarcer, until only the white, gleaming snow covered almost the entire landscape.

On the train were American, Australian, and Dutch tourists, who felt almost equally elated as me at the superb scenery, and when the train made a brief halt at Myrdal, the Dutchmen waved goodbye as they left the train to catch a connection to Flam. At Finse it was just above freezing, and the snow was still banked high outside the station.

And so the journey continued, and by the evening I was once again in Oslo, and with my heavy rucksack on my back, ascended the steep slope to Haraldsheim Youth Hostel, with the air still warm from the bright Spring sunshine. Everywhere was a brilliance of green, nature was truly rejoicing in the initial coming of Spring, a Spring which had been long awaited to the citizens of the North.

After staying two weeks in Oslo, I was more than ever determined to travel to Trondheim, a town I had grown to love more and more with the passage of time. Although it was the end of May, Spring was extremely late in the mountains, and at the old mining town of Roros, high up on the Roros plateau, the birch trees were still quite bare, and it was just as if I had gone back in time.

The train, having crossed the highest point on the Hardanger plateau, slowly descended, and I caught a glimpse of the first signs of green shoots on the dwarf mountain birches. And what a magnificent sight it was as the track followed the course of the river Gaula, with its rushing torrents, high waterfalls cascading through narrow gauges, and forests of tall pine and fir trees. Lower down the river Gaula passed through a region of dense vegetation, with several large, isolated farmsteads, quiet villages, and winding roads which followed closely the lower valley slopes. The temperature rose rather rapidly, and I felt both tired and thirsty.

But how good it was to alight from the train, and walk towards the station exit. How it had changed since I was there 2 years ago, a completely new restaurant, and a very large hall, where one could buy newspapers, fruit, and sweets, book a place on an express train beyond the Arctic Circle, or merely sit down and rest.

And yet the town had changed very little, the fishing smacks were still there, nestling quietly on the placid waters of the harbour, the shops had just closed, and the citizens were making their way home, in a pleasant unhurried manner, by bus, tram, car, or on foot. Both Trondheim and its happy people possessed a dignity unchanged by time.!!

After waiting a few minutes, I boarded a rather empty bus, which quickly became almost full to capacity after making a few stops. It seemed too good to be true, as I approached the youth hostel, and opened the entrance door to the main hall and the reception. The warden, Rolf, was so pleased to meet me, and after a quick shower, I found a tasty meal already made.

Rolf told me that his wife and two sons were spending some of their time in a cottage by the sea, about 12 miles away, and invited me to join them for the evening. How I enjoyed every minute of the journey, the road hugged the rocky coast, and the bright sun was reflected on the calm waters of the Trondheim fjord, it was warm, in fact, it seemed hard to realise that I was only about 250 miles south of the Arctic Circle. Inger, and her sons, Peter and Gunnar, made me so welcome, it happened to be Peter's birthday, we ate fancy cakes, strawberries, and finished up with strong coffee.

Even after the long journey, I still felt fresh, and went for a walk in the nearby forested hillside. Here I was, in my beloved Trondelag, with time to both work, relax and find infinite joy and gratitude amongst such splendid surroundings.!! Late in the evening Rolf drove me back to the hostel, the western sky was a purple glow, the streets of Trondheim were almost completely deserted, and I knew it would not be long before the rich glow of a Norwegian sunset would merge into the friendly dawn of another day.

There was plenty of work to be done in the garden, weeding, and transplanting some of the shrubs planted 2 years ago. I enjoyed my work, but found it demanded great patience. Luckily, a young German, who was eager on hitch-hiking to the North Cape, offered to help, I was only too pleased to have his help for two days, this put my mind at ease, and the bulk of the work was accomplished slightly earlier than anticipated. This also gave me time to help a Norwegian, Karre, and his Finnish wife, Irja, who badly needed work in their garden.

From their garden I had a fine view over the town, there were so many trees and parks that Trondheim looked like a green oasis, stretching down to the blue waters of the Trondheim fjord. Even walking to their home was a joy in itself, passing many old wooden houses, and their attractive gardens, so similar to those in Scotland and Wales. Their son Sverre made me feel at home, he was very fond of animals and worked in a hospital.

One rather chilly Sunday, I decided to visit the unique Ringve music museum. Catching the last remaining tramway which serves Trondheim, I was quickly transported to the precincts of Ringve manor, climbing a hill covered with high grass and thick clumps of woodlands. As I entered the courtyard, my swift pace slackened, and with eager attention I gazed at this home of longstanding historical importance. Clouds hurried swiftly across the bright sunlit sky, turning the hills and woods into an ever-changing scene of rapidly altering colour contrasts.

The oldest part was built about 1650, and here Wessel Tordenskjold of naval fame, lived for many years. Much of the interior is unchanged since then.

Christian Anker Bachke was the last proprietor, he was a business man and Belgian consul in Trondheim. In 1920 he was fortunate enough to marry the Russian born Victoria Rostin, he had the idea of founding a music—museum, and it was she who made his fine idea come true.!!

As Ringve was of historical importance, he decided to preserve it for future generations, and bequeathed the manor to the Norwegian nation, before his death in 1946.

The museum project had been considered as something to evolve sometime in the future, but Victoria Bachke was determined that the "future should be now". She had the courage, patience, and skillful determination to fulfil this tremendous task. Thanks to her active life, imagination, and all-conquering charm she was able to open, in 1950, a museum to Peter Wessel Tordenskjold. And, already in 1952, she was able to open the museum, with hundreds of instruments from all over the World.

To me, the most important ideal of Victoria Bachke, was that she put the instruments in such a way as to create the typical atmosphere of former times. To achieve this, she bought a splendid assortment of furniture, lamps, and other household articles. And nowhere does one read "Please, do not touch", as this would disturb the homely atmosphere of happy, bygone days. Many of the instruments can be played, some of them play tunes from 300 or 150 years ago, or even yesterday.!!

The first room has no musical connection, but is dedicated to Christian Anker Bachke, this was his former office. Close to his picture, on the piano, is that of Mme. Victoria Bachke, taken in her magnificent Russian national costume.

Ringve Manor has been a meeting-place for music-lovers which is witnessed by the array of personally signed photos around the piano. They include such names as Ignaz Triedmann, Lilly Kraus, Paderewski, as well as one of Franz Liszt private pupils Eugened, Albert. In a glass-case, are Christian Bachke's medals and orders, and the picture of the pianiste Theresa Careno, who gave him lasting inspiration.

Since the first dawn of civilisation music has existed, if only in a simple form to begin with, and the first room clearly shows how mankind strives to improvise and improve.

A small sculpture on the wall denotes the Ringve symbol, it is a copy, the original, dating from about 1200 A.D., can be found in Trondheim cathedral. The monk is called "The Fiddler" and the instrument represents Europe's very first bow-instrument, which was already in use in the 7th century. And it originated from Wales, and was called the "Crwth". And this room houses many forms of violins.

There are two extremely fine Hardanger fiddles, these originated about 3 or 4 centuries ago. Even today, they represent an essential part of Norwegian folk-music. The Swedish old violin, the "Nyckelharpa"; and the Norwegian "Langeliek, are also on show. The spinet is rather similar to the piano, but its action and weaker sounds have little in common.

The Mozart room was Ringve's former garden-room. The ceiling and light pastel colours on the walls inspired Mme. Victoria to gather instruments of the rococco period. But, owing to lack of space, she made a place for the historic baroque, so the collection is from the mid. 17th., to 18th., centuries. The spinets came from Hamburg and Florence, one was even made in Prague, before being shipped to South America.

Victoria Bachke was so determined that she even found a splendid harpsicord at the Palace of Versailles, and it now stands under a painting of the Mozart family. It was made in 1737 and still has beautiful tunes when played.

One of the most loved treasures is the pianoforte made in 1777 by the famous Johann Andreas Stein of Augsburg. Mozart praised openly his genius and dedication, today only five such small pianos exist in Europe this is still played at historical concerts.

The Beethoven room consists of instruments of the 19th century. A delicately formed lyre represents the period, both in decorative and practical use. Close to the window is a large brown piano built by Conrad Graf of Vienna. He was a firm friend of Beethoven, and built the master's last piano, which is standing at the Beethoven museum in Bonn. The one in Ringve was the property of a Norwegian family, having been purchased in Vienna and brought to Norway by horse and sledge.

The next room, representing the later 19th century, and the romantic world of Chopin. With its silken tapestries and crystal chandeliers, we are reminded of ladies in crinolines with fans and polka-curls. In an alcove, we can study the artist's death mask and Chopin's sensitive and handsome features, while underneath is a plaster cast of his famous left hand. Several pictures represent this splendid genius, and a photograph, taken in 1849. Although there are no instruments of his, a small card table was transported to Trondheim by Thomas Tellefsen. He was the son of the organist at Trondheim cathedral, he longed to be a student of Chopin and later became an internationally known pianist.

In a corner is a grand piano, of Polish make, which she found in a loft in Trondheim, a truly welcome surprise for one who had travelled so far.

There is also a fascinating collection from all areas of Africa, South and North America, and even Tibet. And perhaps the most primitive of all, the dijeridoo, a long hollow branch which the Australian aboriginals tap with 2 wooden sticks.

Near the staircase I noticed a book which shows handwritten music composed by Mozart, an original, written by Franz Schuberts Father. Above it is the first edition of "Der Wanderer".

One room contains various guitars, from places as far apart as Yugoslavia, Greece, Norway, and France. Of special appeal is the balalaika, for it reminds me so much of the strength and intense fascinating beauty of Russian music, with the hardships and yearnings of the people.!! The zithern from Finland represents the inventive spirit, tenacity, and hard-working honesty of this Northern people.!!

Another room, which takes us back to the eighties, is the Grieg-Tchaikovsky room, for these two composers were contempories and once actually met at Leipzig. On the grand piano is a portrait of Tchaikovsky. Victoria Bachke, having lived 50 years outside her native Russia, visited Moscow, her home town, and visited Tchaikovsky's home at Klin, shortly before his death.

Most of Grieg's personal belongings are at his house at Trollhaugen on the outskirts of Bergen. A few of his personal belongings are on show, and several of his pictures.

Items from the orient and Norwegian instruments show a remarkable variety, and it gives delight to view the room dedicated to Victoria Bachke, especially her splendid Russian national costume.

It was good to be out again in the clear Northern air, and as I walked across the wooded hillside, I realised how much this lady had benefited mankind.!!

While in Trondheim I also visited Aslaug and Erling, a delightful couple who I first met in Gothenburg, I always felt so happy and relaxed at their homely house, only a short walk from the Youth Hostel. And just talking to some of the "locals" in one of the many restaurants, or meeting wanderers at the hostel was a joy in itself. But it was high time to leave Trondheim, even though I would have loved to stay there far longer.

But duty called, and there was work waiting to be done, both in Oslo and Gothenburg.

When the time comes to leave Scandinavia, there remain a multitude of impressions of the splendid landscapes of mountain, forests, lakes, and rivers, sunlit days and starlit nights. And the strong, progressive democracy where employer and employee work together for the common-good. These lands, although not powerful, do much to benefit many other nations, especially towards peace and enlightenment.

Most of all I think of true, lasting friendships with many of the Northern peoples which have become stronger and finer with the passage of time. And the many acts of spontaneous kindness have made my sojourn a festive occasion which has given lasting happiness to all concerned.

And true friendship makes life more nobler, richer and joyous in every way.!!

Tranquil scene in Orebro, Sweden. R.P.

FLOWERS AT FINSE

"The flowers are out at Finse", came the message. Next morning, a warm, sunny one, we travelled on the Express from Bergen to Finse. As we walked in the direction of the azure-scored Hardanger Glacier, the sight that greeted our eyes exceeded all our expectations. Arctic poppies, cranesbills, and the intense blue stars of the Snow Gentian grew beside our path and ahead the ground was studded with candy pink Alpine Catchflies, miniature white "Wood Stars" and deep golden Autumn Hawkbits and many more species. Every year since I have returned to Finse in early August to walk among the mountain flora of the Hardangervidda with joy in my heart.

Finse 1222 is open during August and we enjoy the relaxed, friendly atmosphere of this mountain hotel where we can share for a while the life in the local community at the highest station on the Oslo-Bergen railway. In high summer glacier walking, hiking and cycling replace ski-ing as the main recreation here on Europe's largest mountain plateau.

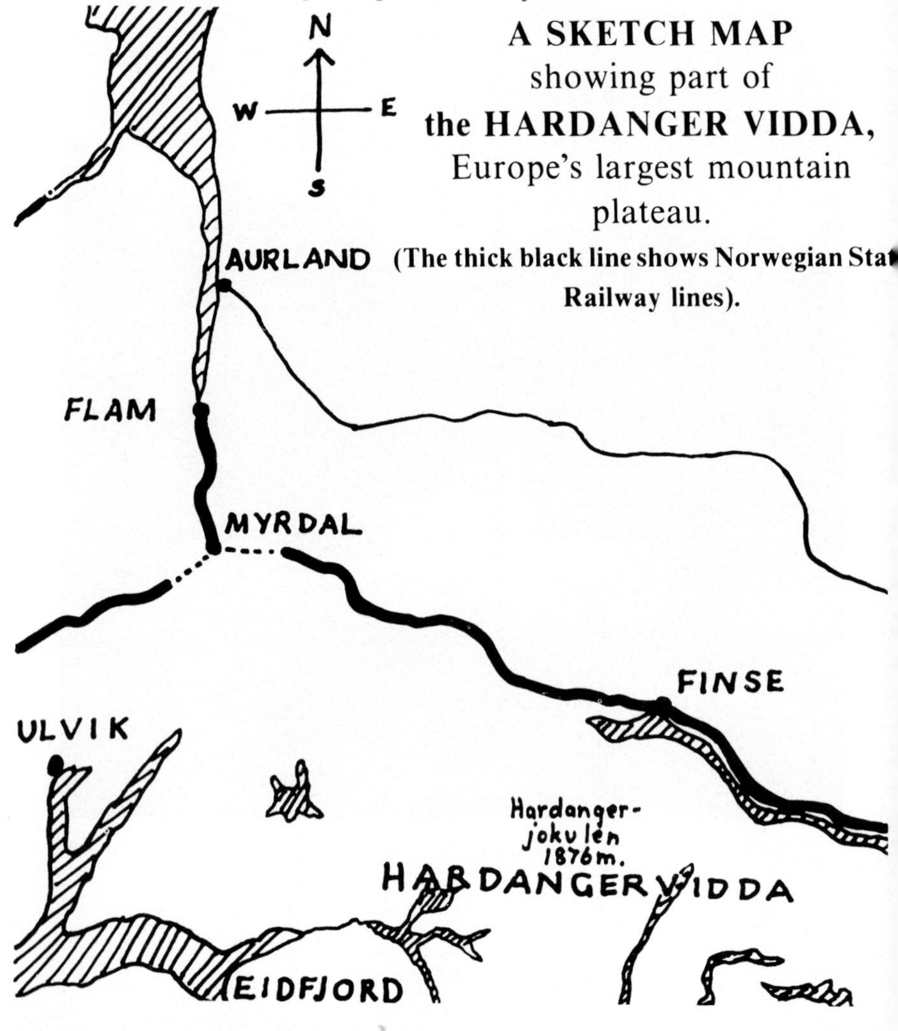

One of the joys of travelling by train in Scandinavia in Summer is the opportunity to see myriads of wild flowers.

In June and July the mauve Wood Cranesbill clothes many banks, a little later there are stretches of carmine Rosebay Willow Herb. Throughout the Summer the clear blue Harebells (the Bluebells of Scotland) abound everywhere. In some areas, including Mydral and Upsete, the tall, purple Monkshood flourishes.

As well as the many common species, a number of rarer ones are to be found on or near the stations. Gentians bloom near one main line junction and the halt at Kjosfossen is a paradise for keen botanists. Among the mountain flowers, Saussurea, Grass of Parnassus, Starry Saxifrage, the orange form of Yellow Saxifrage, Mountain Queen and Melancholy Thistle are just a few that can be seen from a train in Western Norway.

In areas near the tree-line the dark green ground cover, in Summer, is Dwarf Birch and this becomes a rich red in Autumn. The low grey-green growth is Willow. Above the tree-line in places Reindeer Moss colours the rocks sage-green.

As Autumn approaches, the many varieties of berries add colour to the landscape. Clusters of scarlet berries festoon the northern Elder and the fruits of the Rowan become a glowing shade of vermillion, while low on the ground are red Cowberries and Cranberries and black Bearberries, Bilberries and Crowberries. The legendary Cloudberry (Molte in Norwegian) is difficult to find but it does fruit earlier in different places in the mountains.

From the high mountains to the sheltered valleys, Autumn brings a harvest of beauty and colour.

HAREBELL

IDEAS AND IDEALS.

In the stillness of Nature we can gain Inner Peace and Joy in Living.

The greater man's love, the greater his success.

If you desire the best from Life you must believe your Best, not now and then, but always.

Joy in Living!! Joy in Working!! Joy in Friendship!! Joy in Giving!! Joy in Learning.!!

Sincerity makes for Purpose, and Ideals for a greater, happier Way of Life.!!

True Friendship stands the test of time.

The small flower, the immensity of the Universe, radiate Joy and the Abundance of the fuller Life.

Life on Earth, though full of hardships, is an indescribable, splendid occasion.

Man can only learn from the things he loves. *Goethe.*

To live is not enough, we must also have sunshine, freedom, and—a little flower. *H. C. Andersen.*

Cruising the Naeroy Fjord – an awe-inspiring experience.

September reflections at Bakke. R.P.

JOURNEYS IN WESTERN NORWAY

NORWAY IN A NUTSHELL – with the Flåm Railway and a Sogne Fjord Cruise

This spectacular and highly enjoyable round-trip merits pride of place for anyone who wishes to see the splendour of the fjords and mountains of Western Norway. The tour can be easily made from Oslo or Bergen, or the various resorts on the Sogne and Hardanger fjords.

In Bergen we can board the morning train to Voss and Myrdal. Soon the train is speeding past old stately wooden houses nestling on the mountainside with the calm waters of Lundegard to our right. After passing through the five mile long tunnel under Mount Ulriken we make a brief stop at Arna station. Suddenly a fine panorama of the Sorfjord can be seen to our left, and we shall follow this beautiful fjord for several miles. On the opposite side of the fjord the island of Osteroy can be seen, this is the largest inland island in Norway. The fjord is about 2,000 feet deep and 35 miles long. At Takvam there is a superb vista of a series of rugged cliffs and later we observe the old farm at Havretunet, a small cluster of houses round a central court. Havretunet is preserved as a museum, being about 300 years old. Trengereid has a large salmon farm, one of Norway's many successful industries, and Atlantic salmon is even flown as far away as the West Coast of U.S.A.

At Vaksdal is the largest flour mill in the whole of Norway, the grain is imported chiefly from Canada and the Mid-West of U.S.A. Here the Summers are too cool for raising wheat, but further east, oats, rye and barley can be grown as the Summers are warmer. At Stanghelle we leave the Sorfjord and travel inland to Dale, Norway's largest textile centre. The Dale factory exports sweaters, both hand and machine-made, to all parts of the World. Trollkona tunnel, opened in 1988, has shortened the journey from Dale to Bolstadsoyri, where the train runs parallel to the Bolstads river, famous for its salmon fishing. Sometimes a triumphant fisherman can be seen holding up his fine catch.

At Evanger, near the small white church is a memorial which honours the steadfast work and achievements of Knut Nelson, who was born on a hillside farm near here. From 1893 to 1895 he was the Governor of Minnesota becoming the first Scandinavian member of the U.S. Senate. He has truly been called Norway's greatest emigrant to the U.S.A.

After following the swiftly flowing Vosso river we pass Bulken, and at this point, on a clear, calm morning there are superb reflections of the farms, meadows, woods and mountains on the wide expanse of the Vangsvatnet lake. Six miles further on is Voss, and many Norwegians emigrated from this area to North America. Knut Rokne is the best known, he became the Football coach of Notre Dame, in addition he was a brilliant chemist, and prolific writer. Just ahead from the busy station the spire of Voss church can be clearly seen, this church is over 700 years old. Soon we are crossing the road to Vik and Gudvangen. Vik, famous for the Hopperstad Stave Church, is also on the Sogne fjord, the longest and deepest fjord in Norway. As we climb rapidly towards the high mountains the road leading to the Hardanger fjord, the second largest in Norway, can be clearly seen.

During the next hour we climb to a height of almost 3,000 ft. through sparsely populated yet well forested terrain. Most of the journey the line runs close to the Raundals river. At one point it rushes through a steep gorge; the aquamarine blue of the clear water denotes it has a glacial origin. At one farm we sometimes see the sturdy fjord ponies grazing peacefully on a mountain pasture. The fjording, as it is known, has a short, stiff mane with a distinct black streak. Another Norwegian breed is the Dolehest, which is larger and is brown with a black mane.

Between Urdland and Myrdal the stations are roughly on the contour lines, the next one approx 500ft. higher than the previous one. They are all of wooden construction, and their artistic structure blends so well with the spectacular surroundings. At Reimegrend the forest is mainly pine, interspersed with aspen and birch. Mjolfjell station is at the nearest point to the Hardanger fjord from the Bergensbanen, and a steady day's walk would bring one to the popular resort of Ulvik. Mjolfjell derives its name from a nearby mountain (fjell) which looks like flour or meal. Further on we can see below us, at the local halt, Orneberget, the large Mjolfjell youth hostel, popular with Norwegians and others who enjoy hiking amonst the wild mountains. At Upsete we enter the three mile long Gravahalsen tunnel, before arriving at Myrdal station, (altitude 2,845 ft.) which is situated just on the timberline, and partially encircled by high mountains. The view is very dramatic, especially when there is a thick snow cover. The station has a fine, warm waiting room, with a cafeteria which is kept open at the busy season.

Here we change to board the famous Flåm train. The conductors are particularly friendly and helpful, and, like most of the Norwegian railway staff, only too pleased to be of help. The Flåm trains have a specially adapted engine and braking system to descend almost 3,000 ft. in a mere 12.4 miles. The construction was a remarkable engineering feat as the steepest gradient is 1 in 18. The line was commenced in 1920 and finished in 1940. The total length of tunnels is 6km., the most remarkable being the 'reverse' tunnel, with almost a figure of eight within the mountain. There are no bridges on this remarkable line and in three places tunnels for the river have been blasted through the rock face.

As we slowly descend beneath a short series of snowsheds the friendly conductor bids us welcome, remarking that he will inform us of the most interesting places on our journey and tells us something of the Flåm railway.

At Vatnahalsen a brief halt gives us the opportunity to admire the superb surroundings of this hotel. There are no roads here, so it still retains a rather unique setting, being easily reached by train from Oslo and Bergen. Just below us is a deep blue mountain lake and as the track skirts the lake, we can see several mountain huts (hytter) which are served by Reinunga halt. Below Reinunga is a brief glimpse of the mighty Kjosfossen waterfall. Soon the train makes a series of short stops to allow a fine view looking down to the upper part of the Flåm valley. As we continue our steep descent through the reverse tunnel the same view appears on the other side.

Suddenly the train stops by a long wooden platform, and we are allowed to leave the train for a few minutes to enjoy the splendid sight of the mighty Kjosfossen waterfall. This is the highlight of the spectacular Flåm Line, and tourists from all corners of the World lose no time in taking photographs. To the right of the waterfall are the remains of the first hydro-electric power station built about a century ago, the present power station is across the line. In July the beautiful flowers known as Mountain Queen (Saxifrage Cotyledon) can be clearly seen dotting the bare rock face.

As the train again proceeds downwards we can look upwards and see the three levels of the line we have travelled and higher up the Myrdal station and part of the main Oslo-Bergen Railroad. From here too can be seen the zig-zagging work road used during the construction of the Bergen Railroad. Then follows the longest tunnel, the Nali, about three quarters of a mile long. Immediately afterwards can be seen the goat farm at Kardal, used only during the short Summer. Lower down at Blomheller the pastures are used for sheep grazing.

Once again the river is crossed and now we have the views to our right. At Berekvam, the halfway station with a small stretch of double track, the conductor phones to report our arrival and gets permission for us to proceed. Just below the station is a small mountain farm. Only one farm in three is self supporting. The government gives generous subsidies, and often the farmers have another occupation as well.

Before long we make our third and last crossing of the rushing river, and from now on the views will be on our left hand side. The mighty Rjoandefossen waterfall with a free fall of 420 ft., can soon be seen before the train enters the last tunnel of the Flåm Line. As the track gently winds to the right, a superb view of the old part of the village of Flåm, with the beautiful wooden church, built in 1667, is revealed. High above is the peak of the Vibmesnosi mountain. Now we are on more level terrain, with brightly painted houses, well-kept gardens, meadows and smiling orchards. Here too salmon-fishing is very popular during the Summer. Near Lunden station can be seen an early iron-age burial ground. Once again our cheerful conductor announces that we are approaching our destination at Flåm, with the bus and ferry connections. Just to the right is the Brekke farm, and Arne Brekke emigrated from here to the Mid-west of the U.S.A.

The Flåm Line has so much beauty and many contrasts that one journey is hardly sufficient to experience something of this most remarkable and spectacular line.

Flåm is at the head of the Aurlands fjord, an arm of the Sogne fjord, the longest in Norway. It is about 100 miles from the Atlantic and yet seaweed grows by the fjord edge. We have ample time to relax and enjoy a hot meal or simple snack at one of the local cafeterias. We can take a stroll by the fjord, walk by the river or climb the slope to a large rock to enjoy a wonderful view of the fjord and mountains while we watch the fast ferry from Bergen coming in to dock, and the local boat making a Sognefjord cruise. In the late Summer brisling-fishing boats can be seen. Large cruise ships, including the Q.E.2 and S.S. Norway can anchor close to Flåm.

Soon it is time to board the ferry to Gudvangen. As we head down the fjord, we look back to Flåm, and up to Otternes, now a museum. At the small town of Aurland the ferry makes a brief stop to take on more passengers. The 700 year old white-washed old stone church, with its nearby dark wooden bell tower, and the old wharves create a peaceful setting of timeless charm. Aurland has a large factory producing high quality shoes and a hydro-electric power station which supplies the whole of Oslo with electric power. It is interesting to reflect that the population of Flåm and Aurland was greater in the last century as many of the local people emigrated to the U.S.A.

Our next stop is Undredal. Only recently has it been possible to reach it by road, before it the ferry was its only link with the outside World. Our eyes seek out the tiny church, the smallest in use in Scandinavia, as it only seats forty. Built in 1147 as a Stave church, its exterior was altered in 1722. Its interior is still an architectural and cultural gem and a few years ago the Captain of the Balestrand – Flåm ferry took the pleasure of showing us around this much beloved church. Undredal also produces goat cheese, markets raspberries and has a mussel farming enterprise.

Moving northwards we are amazed to see a remote farm high up above the steep rocky cliffs. This inaccessible small-holding was first established in the middle of the sixteenth century and was inhabited until quite recently. The white house replaced an older one and it took five years to build as all the materials had to be carried up from the fjord. Here the ferry turns sharply south to enter the narrowest fjord in the whole of Europe, the Naeroy fjord, below the shadow of a towering cliff. Away to our right, as we turn, the main part of the Sogne fjord stretches to the open sea, nearly 100 miles away. Sometimes we can see the Midtfjords exchange of some passengers between the Gudvangen-Kaupanger ferry and the Flåm-Bergen hydrofoil.

The sheer beauty of the Naeroy fjord with its many waterfalls suspended like white ribbons from the high mountain walls is almost too difficult to describe.

The peaks rise to 4,000 ft. above us, and the fjord is almost as deep. We soon come to a break in the mountain wall and here is Dyrdal, a remote and yet attractive farming and fishing hamlet. Not far away on the opposite shore is a farm with only one resident. Formerly a large family lived here, and it is good to see other members of the family often making a welcome visit. Earlier this century the inner fjord froze over, so horse-drawn sledges were used from here, at Styve farm, to Gudvangen to carry the winter post.

Between here and Tufte sometimes the kobbe (fjord seals) can be seen chasing the sea trout or resting on the rocks. Tufte farm has brought more land into use again and has a thriving herd of goats. On our left the mound of an old Viking tomb can be clearly seen. Bakke has perhaps the most picturesque setting on the Naeroy fjord with its fine stand of spruce trees and the white Bakke church, over a hundred years old. At a recent wedding here many of the participants wore their Sogne costumes.

When we arrive at Gudvangen there is great activity as the passengers stream off the ferry to board the waiting buses and cars prepare to move towards the ferry. There is also time to visit the souvenir and coffee shop before taking the local bus to Voss.

The valley is called Naeroy too, and we follow it besides the river. Ahead runs a scree shaped like a dragon or lizard, and long ago stories were told of this and other valley features such as the hole high up on the Jordalsnuten. The older houses in the village have distinctive patterns above the windows. Before modern transport shortened distances so greatly each community developed its own style of decoration.

The road we travel was once busy with stolkjaerre drawn by sturdy fjordings whenever cruise ships called. They transported the passengers to and from Stalheim, and the stolkjaerre used by Kaiser Wilhelm is preserved in the valley. Towards the head of the valley is the gabbrolite quarry and immediately afterwards our bus crosses the small bridge featured in the opening sequences of the film "Song of Norway". We now suddenly begin to ascend the steepest road in Norway by a series of hairpin bends, the views becoming more and more dramatic as we wind slowly upwards. These bus drivers are highly skilled at driving through all sorts of rugged terrain.

To our right the Sivlefossen pounds from rock to rock while to our left far below the turbulent waters of the Stalheimsfossen can be seen. As the road levels off at the top the kindly driver points out a huge memorial stone dedicated to a renowned Norwegian poet, Per Sivle, who was born on a small farm nearby.

At Stalheim our bus waits for a few minutes, and we make our way through the hotel and across the garden to gaze at a splendid panorama, which was a subject chosen by one of Norway's famous painters, J. C. Dahl. Returning through the lounge we pause to look at two display cases on the wall. On the left is a set of the Hardanger bridal 'regalia' and to the right a Hardanger fiddle. There are many antiques here, including a very early Gutenburg bible. The private open-air museum is open by appointment. As we continue on our journey we pass the large Oppheim lake and the beautiful old wooden churches at Oppheim and Vinje. Sometimes the coach stops so that people can admire the Tvindefossen waterfall. The scenery is now more gentle and everywhere can be seen small farmsteads. Just before entering Voss, on the steep mountainside is a ski-centre with several ski-runs.

In Voss many of the buildings are post-war, but there are older wooden houses too. St. Olav's cross has stood here since 1023. Voss church dates from 1277 and the seven feet thick walls are a tribute to the labour of the local inhabitants. Its dark wooden tower is unusual in design. Here Knut Rockne, the American football coach of Notre Dame, was baptised and just beyond the church we can see a boulder with a bas relief of this noble individual. It is on a lawn just below the slope leading to Voss station. Not far away, high on the hillside is Molstertunet, a cluster of old farms, and two families lived in this 'cluster tun' until 1925. Nearby the purpose-built modern museum shows much of the former ways of life around Voss, and several of the local painter Lars Osa's pictures. Nearby is the cable car 'Hangurbanen' and from the top are superb views over the Vangsvatnet lake and the surroundings of Voss.

Soon it is time to catch the next train to charming, friendly Bergen and just after leaving Voss we have a glimpse of Finneloftet, the oldest secular building in Norway. Many of the vistas we enjoyed this morning have a different beauty lit by the western sun.

We return to Bergen a little tired but happy, having enjoyed some of the most beautiful scenery in the World. There is still time to travel up Floibanen to see the lights come on in Bergen, but perhaps we will leave that until another evening.

Travellers from Oslo may enjoy 'Norway in a Nutshell' as part of their journey from Oslo to Voss or Bergen, or return overnight from Voss or Bergen, reaching Oslo by early morning.

Those who wish to see the Flåm Railway and cruise on the fjords and return the same evening to Oslo may take the excursion known as 'The Sogne Fjord Cruise – A scenic experience'. They will travel on the early morning train to Myrdal and down the Flåm railway to board a boat to cruise along the Aurlands and Naeroy fjords returning to Aurland in time to catch the bus to Geilo to connect with the evening train to Oslo.

Hol's colourful annual Festival, Hallingdal.

Panorama of Naeroy Valley from Stalheim.

Through the summer Skibladner cruises regularly between Eidsvoll, Hamar and Lillehammer.

Lillehammer – before the tremendous changes made for the 1994 Winter Olympics.

BERGEN

This is my favourite city in Norway and over many years I have grown to like it more and more. May I stress, "Take time to enjoy the feel of Bergen." The city centre, set amid high mountains on the beautiful Bergen fjord, is a lovely place to wander, wide streets with large stores, fine parks and narrow streets of traditional wooden houses are all close to the Bryggen, (an UNESCO site of special interest) with the Hanseatic houses and nearby the lively fish and flower markets.

Behind the Bryggen the funicular railway climbs the steep wooded slopes of Mt. Floien. From the end station there are fine views over the heart of Bergen and the fjord to the islands beyond. A beautiful sunset viewed from Floien is a memorable experience. From the funicular there are pleasant walks through the mountain forest and beside the lakes which are Bergen's reservoir. Lower down are narrow streets with fascinatingly diverse wooden houses, lovingly preserved. A stroll along these affords many interesting viewpoints.

Below are the spires of the Cathedral and the seventeenth century Korskirke Church, and further towards the west the twin towers of St. Mary's Church, (Bergen's oldest building) one of the loveliest of the Romanesque churches in Norway, built in the early part of the 12th century. Towards the mouth of the harbour lies the Rosenkrantz Tower and Haakonshall.

Maybe Bergen's best known church is the Fantoft Stave Church which was transported to its present site from Fortun near the Luster fjord in the last century. This may be reached by bus on a city tour or from the bus station.

Bergen is justly proud of the aquarium, where besides the many fish on view, there are penguins and seals to observe. The museums and art galleries appeal to a wide variety of tastes. The Hanseatic Museum, Bryggen Museum and Gamle Bergen, give a vivid picture of life in earlier times.

The evenings provide a wealth of musical and theatrical experience during the International Musical Festival and from time to time during the year. There are concerts at both Troldhaugen and Lysoen, Ole Bull's villa. Fana Folklore and Bergen Folklore give a good insight into the rich and varied Norwegian folk culture.

Day excursions, "Norway in a Nutshell" and "The Hardanger Fjord" are the most popular. These tours can easily be done by public transport. Fast comfortable hydrofoils link Bergen with Stavanger, with some interesting calls en route, including Haugesund and the island of Karmoy. A two or three day tour we specially recommend is to Nordfjord by steamer. This enables one to cruise along the coast with calls at Floro, Maloy and Sandane before visiting Stryn and the Briksdal Glacier.

VOSS – HARDANGER – SETESDAL – KRISTIANSAND

The journey Voss to Valle gave us a wonderful variety of scenery. We started along the scenic route to Ulvik and twisted down Skjervet with the falls in full spate, then we veered south to Bruravik to board the ferry at Brimnes. As we crossed the Hardanger fjord the view was splendid. To our left the Osafjord stretched away to Osa and Ulvik, a popular port of call for cruise ships, and as we neared Brimnes we looked up the Eidfjord. Away to our right along the north shore lay Kvanndal, with its longer ferry crossing to Utne and Kinsarvik, and bus connections along the north shore to Alvik, Oystese and Norheimsund.

From Brimnes we continued along the fjord's edge via Kinsarvik with its old Viking dock, and Ullensvang, where the little hut in which Grieg composed is preserved, to Odda. Travelling past orchards festooned with bright red apples we had marvellous views of the Folgefonn glacier across the Sorfjord. At one point the view brought vividly to mind the gifted old painting "Hardanger Wedding" by Gude and Tidemand.

Our route continued via Roldal, with its historic church, long a place of pilgrimage, set in a green valley below us. Passing the lake we climbed to cross the south eastern fringe of the Hardangervidda, brilliant with Autumn colour in early September, to Haukeliseter, a cluster of traditional wooden houses, above a glittering blue mountain lake, and so through Haukeligrend to Hovden. We checked in at the delightful youth hostel near the Hovden mountain hotel and continued on the bus to Valle via Bykle with its tiny church and beautifully carved stabbur.

On this sunny afternoon Valle was so peaceful. The farmers were busy in the fields at the end of a good harvest, and we seemed to have the place to ourselves until a friendly group of young skateboarders appeared.

As the sun slowly set we relaxed and enjoyed a meal at the welcoming cafeteria before boarding the local bus for Hovden. The colours of the evening sky were intense as we travelled past lonely lakes and woods. The bus driver was most helpful, just like so many of the friendly Norwegians, and make a long detour to set us down just outside our warm cabin. Above the stars twinkled brightly in the clear mountain atmosphere.

Very early next morning the same bus collected us and driving south as dawn was slowly breaking we saw an elk (moose) and later a roe deer. Along the valley we passed some of the traditional silversmiths whose fine work is a feature of the Setesdal. Near Evje we became a "school bus" and enjoyed the company of many flaxen-haired youngsters.

Arriving in Kristiansand we enjoyed "brunch" at a local store. The bus and rail station are close to the quays and the city centre.

SOME CITIES AND TOWNS IN DENMARK

Copenhagen is a city with so much to see and do, and each will find his or her own list of "musts". The Central Tourist Information Office in Copenhagen is extremely helpful and well stocked with informative material. It faces the City Hall.

City Hall Square (Radhüspladsen) is the lively centre of the city. Nearby is Stroget with many delightful streets and squares. A walk along its length brings one to Nyhavn. On my first visit I watched the fisherwomen in traditional garb selling fish by the statue of the fisherwoman.

Central Copenhagen has many spires and towers, including the one atop the City Hall. These are good landmarks and one quickly learns to recognise them. Vor Frelsers Church has the spiral spire, and the distinctive spire of dragon's tails is on the Stock Exchange. The Round Tower, an astronomical observatory dates from 1642.

The Home of Her Majesty Queen Margarethe is Amalienborg Palace. Rosenborg Palace is the Royal Museum and has lovely gardens. The Parliament is housed in Christianborg Palace.

One can learn much about Danish history in interesting ways in the National Museum. Ny Carlsberg Glyptoteket is famous for the collection of Etruscan, Greek, and Egyptian antiquities as well as some outstanding French impressionist art.

Copenhagen's most famous piece of sculpture must be the Little Mermaid. You will find her on a rock at the water's edge. She is easy to find if one walks southwards from Amalienborg Palace.

Just across the road from the main railway station is Tivoli Gardens. The tower there is a Chinese pagoda. It is a delightful place to spend an enjoyable evening.

Hillerod is about half an hour's journey north of Copenhagen. It is a friendly small town with good shops but its great attraction is the Frederiksborg Castle. The rich interior of this imposing castle is fascinating to visit, but the dramatic silhouette of the building is best viewed across the lake. We enjoyed a Saturday morning folk dancing display, in aid of a local charity, in the park, with Frederiksborg as a backdrop.

North of Hillerod is Fredensborg, quite different in character with its pale walls and black roof. This lovely home is used by the Royal Family in Spring and Autumn. During July the gardens are open to the public and are a delight.

East from here is Lousiana, easily reached from the station at Humleback. Devotees of modern art will make for this attractive gallery.

Helsingor is at the end of the line from Copenhagen. Its Kronberg Castle is the Elsinore of Hamlet, made famous by its Shakespeare connection, but Denmark has many more beautiful and interesting castles. A frequent ferry connects to Helsingborg in Sweden, and rail and car passengers continue their journeys north and east from here.

Just a short journey from Copenhagen, on the main route to Odense and Jutland, brings us to Roskilde. On our way from the station the konditori with the wonderful aroma from their tastefully displayed confections proved irresistible.

Next we found the towering red brick Cathedral and entered what was to us an amazing mausoleum. Here centuries of Danish history can be studied but to study the Viking Age head for the Viking Ships Museum, an imaginatively presented display of the exciting finds made in 1957.

The train journey from Roskilde to Odense includes the comfortable ferry crossing Korsor-Nyborg and gives one another view of life in Denmark, a country that is a collection of islands with a peninsula. This is just one of the many ferry crossings and pleasure cruises one can take in Danish waters.

Odense, in spite of today being quite an industrial city, has a beautiful old quarter with Hans Christian Andersen's house and museum. It was a delight to share the pleasure of Danish children at the museum.

Near the station is the bus station and the Danish State Railway Museum which I found very interesting. Odense is the third largest city in Denmark.

Situated on the east coast of the Jutland peninsula, Aarhus is the second largest city, and is highly industrialised with a large seaport. It takes about five hours by train from Copenhagen. Of special interest is "Den Gamle By", an open-air museum with fifty buildings spanning the years 1500 to 1850. There are other museums too, such as the Fire-fighting Museum, the Press Museum, and one covering the time from the Stone Age to Viking times. The crypt of Vor Frue Church, from 1060, is Scandinavia's oldest church. Queen Margarethe has her summer residence in Marsekisborg Palace.

Not far from the busy ferry port of Frederikshavn is Aalborg, on the north-east coast of Jutland. The Aalborg Tower gives a fine view of the highly industrialised city.

Just east of the main road south of Aalborg. Rebild Bakker is a national park given by Danish-Americans in 1912. Amidst its heather-clad slopes special 4th July celebrations are an annual event. Lincoln Log Cabin houses the Danish Emigration Museum.

Poseidon overlooks Kungsport Avenue, one of Gothenburg's fine boulevards.

Lennard

Danish Tourist Board

Stroget in the heart of cosmopolitan Copenhagen.

Lennard

Danish Tourist Board

The beauty of Danish architecture in Aarhus Old Town.

The splendour of Helsinki's Cathedral.

The busy flower market in Finland's capital.

Sunne Church seen across the Frykensdalen Railway. Only a few miles from here is the KINSHIP MEMORIAL to all those from Varmland who sought and found new homes in America and to the many industrious Finns who settled in this province.

R.P.

The home in Mora of ANDERS ZORN who did much to keep alive the folklore traditions of Dalarna. R.P.

Old world charm in the heart of Dalarnna, beside Lake Siljan, Rattvik church is still flanked by Kyrkstallarna.

Strawberry time in Stavanger.

Home from the fields. Valle in Setesdal. R.P.

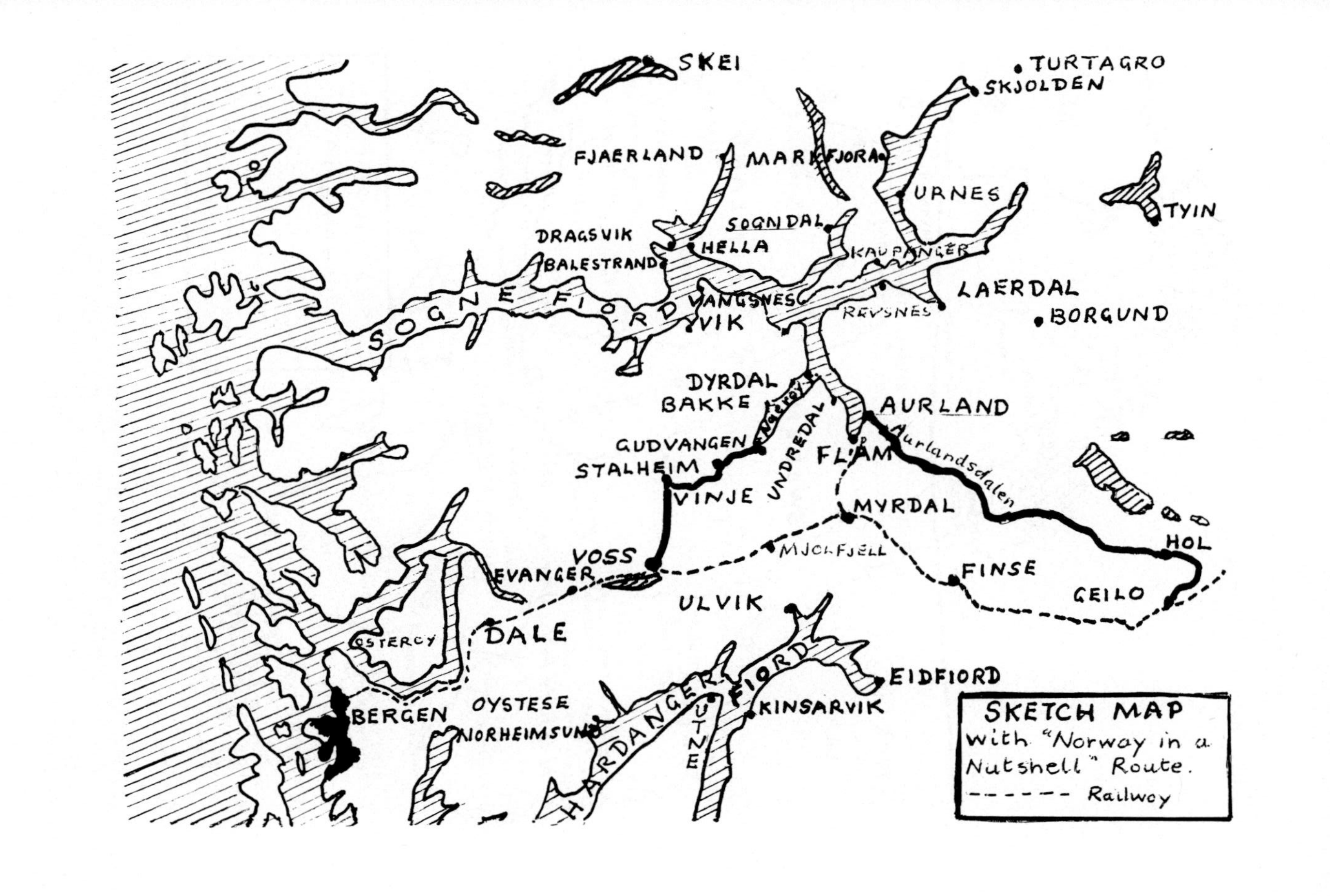
SKETCH MAP
with "Norway in a Nutshell" Route.
- - - - - Railway
SKEI
TURTAGRO
SKJOLDEN
FJAERLAND
TYIN
URNES
SOGNDAL
DRAGSVIK
HELLA
BALESTRAND
KAUPANGER
LAERDAL
BORGUND
SOGNE FIORD
VANGSNES
VIK
REVSNES
DYRDAL
BAKKE
AURLAND
GUDVANGEN
STALHEIM
UNDREDAL
FLÅM
Aurlandsdalen
VINJE
MYRDAL
MJOLFJELL
HOL
VOSS
FINSE
EVANGER
GEILO
ULVIK
DALE
OSTEROY
EIDFIORD
OYSTESE
BERGEN
NORHEIMSUND
KINSARVIK
UTNE
HARDANGER FIORD

NORTH CAPE
VARDO
HAMMERFEST
KIRKENES
TROMSO
LOFOTEN ISLES
NARVIK
SOLVAER
ABISKO
KIRUNA
KOLARI
BODO
FAUSKE
ARCTIC CIRCLE
GALLIVARE
ROVANEMI
U
S
S
R
NORTH
SEA
BODEN
TORNIO
KEMI
LULEA
OULU
GULF OF BOTHNIA
KAJAANI
SWEDEN
FINLAND
KRISTIANSUND
TRONDHEIM
OSTERSUND
UMEA
ALESUND
MOLDE
ANDALSNES
GEIRANGER
DOMBAS
ROROS
VASA
SEINÄJOKI
JOENSUU
SUNDSVALL
SAVONLINNA
OTTA
RINGEBU
PARIKKALA
PORI
FLAM
FAGERNES
TAMPERE
IMATRA
VOSS
MYRDAL
LILLEHAMMER
MORA
RATTVIK
LAHTI
BERGEN
FINSE
GJOVIK
NORWAY
BORLANGE
GAVLE
TURKU
KOTKA
OSLO
SUNNE
UPPSALA
ALAND ISLANDS
HELSINKI
HANKO
VALLE
STAVANGER
SKIEN
KARLSTAD
STOCKHOLM
L. VANERN
L. VATTERN
KRISTIANSAND
BALTIC SEA
HIRTSHALS
FREDERIKSHAVN
GOTHENBURG
JONKOPING
VISBY
AALBORG
VÄXJO
DENMARK
AARHUS
KALMAR
HELSINGER
HALSINGBORG
FREDERICIA
MALMO
ESBJERG
COPENHAGEN
ODENSE
SKETCH MAP OF SCANDINAVIA
Only very few of Scandinavia's many islands and lakes can be indicated on a map on this scale. Finland alone has 187,888 lakes.

MORE ABOUT SWEDEN

GOTHENBURG

Gothenburg is worthy of at least one or two days' visit. Tree-lined avenues, winding canals and gracious buildings give the city a special atmosphere, enhanced by the cheerful friendliness of her citizens.

From Gothenburg it is a short bus ride to Kungalv, a small town with charmingly preserved old streets close to the well sited castle, Bohus Fastning, and a well designed shopping centre. There are frequent trains to Alingsas, an attractive old town to the east, and the resorts along the Bohuslan coast are easy to reach by bus and train. Marstrand is a special favourite, Smogen is an old fishing village and Stromstad, a yachting centre, is the terminus of the scenic coastal railway line. Karlstad, the jewel of the beautiful province of Värmland is also easily reached by rail on a day visit.

DALARNA

Dalarna (Dalecaria) to the north of Varmland is known as the folklore province. Along the shores of Lake Siljan we have visited Leksand, Rattvik and Mora each with a quality of its own. At Midsummer the celebrations there are rich in tradition, as are the church-boat races in July. Mora has Anders Zorn's home and studio. The red Dalarna horses are made at Nusnas near Mora but the yellow ones are produced in Leksand.

Falun is a pleasant town set in lovely countryside jewelled with many lakes. Copper mining began here in the 11th century. There are tours of the old mine, and a mining museum to visit. For us the main attraction was the home of Carl Larsson at Sundborn, a short bus ride from the railway station. We visited this place of great beauty and quiet charm on a glorious September day when the brilliant Autumn colours were at their very best. A charming guide made our visit even more enjoyable. There were so many features that were familiar from the artist's pictures.

SKANE

Skane province, in the far south of Sweden, has Lund, a small yet attractive university city with a beautiful Romanesque Cathedral, and Malmo, the third largest city in Sweden. Malmo boasts fine shops, impressive buildings and beautiful parks. It is less than an hour by hydrofoil from Denmark's capital.

The city is a good centre for visiting the numerous castles and villages of Skane. An hour south of Malmo, through acres of sugar beet, lie the twin villages of Falsterbo and Skanor, idyllic behind their white beaches. In late September this peninsula is on the flight path of millions of migrating birds, and we spent a splendid day observing them.

SMALAND

Smaland province is renowned for glass-making. In Vaxjo there is an excellent museum devoted to the Emigration to North America.

MORE ABOUT SOUTHERN FINLAND

HELSINKI

This Nordic capital lies much farther east than the others and has a unique atmosphere. From the harbour there are regular boats to Tallinn in Estonia, and each day one can travel by train to Leningrad. Her people are friendly, cheerful and confident and so many of them dress with style.

The city's architecture is impressive, and the Senate Square, with the Cathedral, has a wonderful feeling of space. It was designed as an entity by Engel. A short walk to the waterfront brings one to the market square with its busy stalls. Across to the east is the distinctive skyline of the Greek Orthodox Uspensky Cathedral. Both the Academic Bookshop and the splendid Finlandia Hall were designed by Alvar Aalto. The Church at the Temple Square has a startling design by the Suomalainens, and in a different way so has Eila Hiltunen's Sibelius Monument in the park of the same name. Helsinki has many museums and art galleries which the city brochures describe well.

TURKU

This is Finland's third largest city and a large port. It is pleasant to walk along the banks of the Aura River and close to the river is the City's Tourist Information Office where one can collect an excellent map with descriptions of the points of interest along the river. The large shops are near the Market Square, and the city has a number of museums. From Turku there are fast trains to Helsinki and Tampere, Finland's second largest city which is an ideal centre for exploring southern Finland.

SAVONLINNA

Savonlinna is on Lake Saimaa in eastern Finland. We crossed the long winding Punkaharju ridge with magnificent stands of lofty pine trees and glittering water on either side before reaching the outskirts of Savonlinna. As our train approached the small station there was an unexpected view of the mighty Olavinlinna castle, built in the fifteenth century. Walking through the centre of Savonlinna, we passed several boats bearing the names of operas performed in the Summer Opera Festival.

Reaching the floating bridge leading to the castle we stopped to admire the strong lines of this huge fortress. As we did so, the bridge swung aside to allow a Soviet timber boat to glide by. When the bridge was in place again we crossed to explore the castle. What a setting for an opera or concert. No wonder people come from far and wide to share in the experience.

INDEX OF PLACE NAMES

NORWAY

The letters Ø and Å come at the end of the Norwegian alphabet but are indexed here as O and A.

DENMARK

FINLAND

SWEDEN

USEFUL ADDRESSES

Danish Tourist Board
Sceptre House
169, Regent Street
London W1R 8PY

Norwegian Tourist Board
Charles House
5-11, Lower Regent Street
London SW14 4LX

Finnish Tourist Board
Greener House
66-68, Haymarket
London SW1Y 4RF

Scandinavian Tourist Board
655, 3rd Avenue
New York NY10017
U.S.A.

Swedish National Tourist Office
3, Cork Street
London W1X 1HA

For large scale maps of Scandinavia:
Edward Stanford Ltd. (Booksellers)
12-14, Long Acre
London WC2E 9LP

AMENDMENT

Page 39 Oslo East Station is now Oslo Sentral Station.

ERRATA

Page 79 Please read Torniojoki for Tornetrask.
Page 88 Please read Dovre Mountains for Hardanger Plateau.